LEFTOVER LIFE TO KILL

CAITLIN THOMAS

LEFTOVER LIFE
TO KILL

PUTNAM
42 GREAT RUSSELL STREET
LONDON MCMLVII

First published May 1957
Reprinted June 1957

Made in Great Britain and printed
by Ebenezer Baylis & Son Limited,
The Trinity Press, Worcester

I make this in a warring absence

LEFTOVER LIFE TO KILL

AND that is mine: how infinitely preferable and so much
more praiseworthy to be the first to go! The plucked
cabbage stalks, in the wan back garden, confront me
dismally; nature is great at rubbing it in; such a speaking
likeness to my mood of pure uncompromising abandon.
Not a whole life: the better in theory, and I hope the
longest, half is done. For better or for worse, mostly
worse. Only the lesser declining half is left. What shall I
do with this cumbersome object that nobody wants? It is
no good gracefully reclining on the old abused stooge of
indispensability; even the most adored, and unique
people, whom to lose seems impossible: a positive whip-
lash in the face of the human spirit; even they are not
indispensable, once they have gone. And when I see,
with my own two eyes, the gross and indecent speed with
which the momentary cavity is staunched and made fast;
with any handy courage and garbage of rhapsodical talk;
then it would look hardly worth me flustering myself into
a sweat of perturbation over my barely perceptible
scratch on the earth's hard surface.

Nevertheless it is me, and for that reason alone,
important to me. Is there any more terrifying thought
than, once me always me: unless you belong to that
fortunate dolt category that positively exults in being
not only their own true, sweet selves, but always the
same; the greatest compliment of worth in Wales. And
whichever way I turn, writhe, bluff, put on farcical dis-

guises, dedicate myself to blindly shining higher missions whose purpose is holy sacrificial of me, but nebulously ambiguous when pinned down, it is as clear as creeping grey unwelcome daylight, that I have no function in the world whatever.

I just wonder how much more laborious waste am I expected to perpetrate; because the simplest automatic task, like swabbing a table, is a major scientific problem to me, with all the slow wits chugging at the one and only method of perfecting swabbing; and for what? I notice other people are not bothered by this kind of moron's hold-up in their work. And when an hour passes unchecked, instead of rigorously dinning in and jotting down the minutes, it is with a sense almost of triumph that I think: 'I killed that one humanely,' as though my dearest wish were to hurry up the process of time. Quite forgetting where I am so dementedly hurrying, and the ravages entailed on the halcyon graveward journey.

But, if I have got nothing and am going nowhere, why all the noise, the discontent, the restless chewing, the ceaseless searching after a far-away and nameless, yet warmly satisfying, state: a cross between the inviolability of the womb, and the peak of creative elation; which under no known concentration of circumstances could possibly come about: or at least only once or twice in a lifetime. And why all the unnecessary quarrelling, arguing, laying down the law, moralizing, which nobody cares one way or the other about so long as they can have their own little say too. What an inheritance, and where does it come from?

And why not settle down, and be my age, as those charming friends so pointedly insinuate; in fact, patiently resign myself (resignation, perhaps the most stifling word in the language). But how is it done, and to what? I can merely envisage a broody hen sitting, fiercely

8

depressed, on her eggs; ready to attack the first stray visitor; and what if there are no eggs to sit on? So I am led to understand that the above condition of atrophied coma is fitting and desirable for a woman of my years: clucking and preening, fluffing up her breast enviably stuffed with the feathers of virtue, locked with the claws of respectability. What makes her the terror of the coop, so much more deliriously young, than the sluggish, pudding young, is the whiff of decay forever singeing the tips of her wings and tugging at her tail. It is not surprising that she bursts into hectic, last-fling bloom; exploding seeds like an overripe sunflower.

And however much I stare, however doggedly, into the idiotic mug of death: it is impossible to live alone as long as I have without becoming most familiarly aware of that pompous bore always sniffing around, and sticking his dull cold nose into everything; and never going; still I am unable, mentally incapable, of relating the dead thing, the broken body refusing to divulge why or where the occupant has gone, to the thing that was alive. There is no touchable link between the two.

The same endearing, childish hair; the heavy hulk-shaped head; the small, delicate, elongated, utterly useless, hands, that I used to call fins or mitts: there was a definite connection with the fish family. Perhaps they were the nearest, and hardest to understand, to bear; so placidly inactive. And all the innocence was back; he was unborn again; and the barnacled accumulations through the years of good and evil, and corruption, and salvation; the manure that makes a character, had gone. Entirely gone.

Dylan and dying, Dylan and dying, they don't go together; or is it that they were bound to go together; he said so often enough, but I did not heed him. I was as foolish as women are supposed to be, the traditional

9

woman, paid no attention, took him for granted, was only concerned with how to express my own aggressive, demanding, frustrated, vile, jealous self. And look what he has done to me! How brutally cruelly am I punished; surely out of proportion to my misdoing. Let this be a lesson to all rebellious wives; but poor comfort to me.

By such devilish devices, you'd swear there was some-body behind it with the lowest intentions; my rindy fruit of bitterness, already installed since childhood, though I can trace no evidence of suppression—it might have been more salutary had I been suppressed earlier and more thoroughly—swells to top-heavy proportions; dwarfs the happy landscape, colours with venom the smiling peasant. It even darkens the sun, pressing a ferocious torpor down behind my eye-pit sinews. My bitterness is not an abstract substance, it is as solid as a Christmas cake; I can cut it in slices and hand it round and there is still plenty left, for tomorrow.

You have only to look at my hands; the very reverse of Dylan's; square, gnarled, awkward, unwieldy, chunks of flesh; as though born to the soil, and only fit for planting spuds. And the nails: a shameful reproduction of my mind: torn, bitten, bleeding; the dead skin un-furling in grotesque corrugations. My worst vice at the bottom of all my troubles, and disquietingly part of me. And I fail to stop; and God knows I've tried.

They say; that horrible they, who are they? They say confession is a great relief, as liberating and loosening as a flood of tears, to the confessor. I don't agree—I find it unmitigatedly painful; a rough-going gallop that leaves me limp and expended.

And how is it that this 'they' embodies the worst instincts of the community: of petty persecution? I am a permanent victim of their spite, because I do openly what they do in hiding; there is no worse sin to them than the flouting of conventions; what is not seen does not exist.

Does the perversity of my nature now dare complain that:—having carefully and methodically cut off all family ties, deliberately antagonized friends; and made myself generally as intractable, offensive, violent, and as similar to an infuriated wild boar from the horniest jungle as I know how, and that is something I do know about—that I am ostracized? It does. That I have no friends? It does. That nobody loves me? It does. Can insanity go further than that? All for the sake of the mythical, majestic, mountainous furrow I am supposed to be ploughing in my little stagnant ditch of endeavour.

Then when I get a good old-fashioned kick in the teeth, the first thing I do is start snivelling for friends, blubbering and puking for mother; and all the distant, dimly remembered, soothing comforters of my indignantly shunned past. Every bone in my body aches individually with a dragging weariness of pain, and the joints cry aloud for a warm balm; honeyed oil, to be poured, engulfing me, into the rusty sockets. Soporifics, drugs, nectars, elixirs, etc., I want them all; anything to transform me, to make me different, to forget myself even for a second.

But they only make me worse afterwards, when I come to, marooned on an island of reverberating drink; untouchable, unclean as a leper with my little bell of pain, which tinkles so intently with the insistence of an alarm on waking.

He said he loved me; that I was the only woman for him; and, whatever the evidence to the contrary, I believed him, and still do; and I am grateful for that important bit of faith. There is, happily, no limit to the faith of human nature in believing what it wants to believe. But the sudden removal of such a love, such a special love, on such an immortal scale, and the only one, was bound to cause a dropping out of the bottom of my all-in-Dylan world.

I I

IT is one thing starting a new life in the first flush of
omnipotent ambition, when the constellations are laid
out in tempting rows, awaiting your pleasure. Another
altogether when the breath of discord, disappointment,
disillusion has fused through your veins, and discoloured
your blood; leaving, in its sooty passage, a black choked
chimney.

But gradually, through sheer stubborn persistence, in
the jaws of your unwillingness to move, stale repetition
of once-upon-a-time thoughtless motions, forever widen-
ing the gap between it and you, in matchstick stages; a
fragile pattern emerges, with no foundations, the
semblance of a floating name, barely distinguishable in
the enveloping mists, and as ephemeral. All your
instincts long to crush, to pull down to the ground, to
trample on, this skeleton taunt, feebly etched in the sky,
and as wavering as an infant's first pothooks. But as
often as you do—and my vision was precariously on the
verge of submersion—it means starting all over again,
from the grinding beginning.

Slog, plod, shuffle, shamble: boot by blunt-toed boot,
dragging the convict's clanging chains, round and round
the trodden yard. And so it goes on: up, for a gasping,
breathing spell. Down, for an eternity of drowning. The
trouble with drowning is that it is always too temporary;
never lasts long enough; and oh, the tearing awakening!
The never, never agains. The solemn vows, the hell of the

13

hook that fishes you out; the ardent protestations of eternal abstinence.

As to methods of drowning, there are, broadly speaking, three main categories: drink, drugs, sex; or all three together; though they are apt to obliterate each other. Drink: I must talk fast, or drink will be talking about me; it is either good or bad, and when it gets bad, lay off.

Drugs: one of the few vices I have not dabbled in, owing to lack of opportunities; except for the bliss of sleeping pills, which I wish would prolong night into day, and day into night.

Sex: a distastefully more ticklish subject, on which I am sure I have no right to speak, not that such a small consideration will stop me plunging into it up to the quivering nostrils. I can never determine, first of all, what sex, if any, I am; though I am led to believe there is no doubt, in some people's minds, as to my super bitchery. I should prefer to call it pitting of wits, in cases of dire necessity. I have the overdressed townsman's gaucherie, when he is conducted round a farm, up to his knees in dung, and prods the pigs' pubic backs, with a mixture of hysterical affability and distaste; when I am brought, battling as usual, face to face with this very singular, slightly farcical, occasionally nice; and, once in a blue moon, unselfconscious, strange phenomenon. It is so hard to keep one's mind on the matter in hand: it keeps wandering off; into the larder in search of something tasty to eat: busily planning a new incomparable dress; or merely gazing detachedly at the heaving disconnected object getting so puffed up over so insignificant a pussy trifle, as far away, intimately, as the legendary goat-legged satyrs. It is most tantalizing; and not an effective antidote.

I am afraid I have lived too long in this flat, sour, watery country, which suffers from a chronic indigestion of the emotions: they get stuck so far, in a tight ball of heartburn, and unconditionally refuse to be shifted backwards or forwards without an earthquake of change; to be able to respond in the approved manner. Hence the predilection of the English for going abroad, and taking an emotional loosening-up course; to liberate that precious ecstasy which has to be bottled and boxed into words and poetry, in their own grim homeland. No doubt creating our noble traditions, etc.: but not such enormous fun to live among.

The brute facts are, whether you like them or not, and nobody gets drunk on the smell of work, that sweated labour is the only authentic builder. All the intervening diversions or dissimulations only serve to put off the necessity of picking up the humdrum tools yourself; brush, broom, shovel or pencil; and fashioning an object out of your own muddied dregs; even if it is no more than a fumbled one-eyed potato.

That is why I am so sceptical of the holiday abroad convention: 'Just lie in the sun, dear, and relax;' how easy to say; but as soon ask me to relax as ask a cork bobbing in the tempestuous waves to give up its futile efforts and sink tranquilly to the bottom of the sea.

Which accounts for my morbid perversity in staying in this moist, smothering, lost bog-hole, stiff with beautiful inertia, romantic nostalgias; and crass lazy people: they are sunk between the worship of pennies and the decadence of initiative. Even lovable people, some of them; but these are the exceptions to the narrow, sly, keen, prodding-fingered, always counting the cost Welsh. Their most compulsive motive is fear: fear of the elements: key the door quick against the thieving night; fear of the neighbours: what will the *neigh*bours say? precisely that; fear of en*joy*ment: they roll the word round their lascivious tongues with condemnatory gusto.

Death alone is not feared, but courted as a blossoming bride, ardently coveted.

Weddings are tame domestic occasions compared to the impassioned fuss and orgiastic celebrations of a funeral; and whatever worm unsung in begrudged life dies, he is immediately held aloft, before shamed, healthy mankind, as a pedestalled example of unimpeachable sanctity. And if, more gloriously still, he has left behind him a glorious token of his identity and riches, his glory exceeds all bounds.

But there is a pronounced stress and prodding approval on the behind, under the counter and side-door furtiveness. It is the ultimate peak of genteel nicety to carry babies behind; and, as with the figure deformations of fashion, it can actually, by the sheer zeal of aspiring desire, be done, thus obviating the unseemly, crudely unapologetic, almost boastful bulge in front. And if a friend buys a new 'costume', the imperatively correct uniform, preferably pin-striped, or shiny black or 'navy' for all social occasions in these pastoral parts, their first reaction without a glance at the showy, frivolous front is: 'Let's see the *back*.'

Here: in this city of lying down lying, in this city of unheard laughter, in this city of deadpan Laugharne, I chose of my own free will, if indeed I had any will at all, to stay. I had not the courage yet to brave foreign intrusions into my damp secluded cave of pampered private dragons. Not the harsh dazzlement of Italy, exposing me, probing into me, telling shameful tales about me: not yet.

I did it, not with any dazzling idea driving me forward, the very reverse: blindly, intuitively, as a sick animal seeks the concealing shade of hedges, the leafy obscurity of ditches.

On my long dreamwalking tramps into marshy

16

estuary wastes, with always a tickling cobweb of moisture forever brushing over my face, I had to fight, with all the snuffed might of my scattered wits, the almost voluptuous desire to lie down. To sprawl on to some grassy sea-shaped bank, cast up, forgotten drift-wood, and never get up again. My feet visibly dragged; as though weighed down with iron boots, and my skin shrank and puckered as though with the gooseflesh of entering unknown torture rooms: shrinking with pain is not an invention either; in tuned anticipation of the soundlessly drumming, repercussing blows. My head tossed momentarily above the battering waves, like a horse's frantic mane craning towards the shore that was no longer there; and my bleary, detached salt-drenched eyes failed to be detached at all any more.

How far the physical is governed by the mental state had never been rammed into me so brutally before, and the necessity, if indeed there was any necessity in pro-longing this tail between the legs of life, of forcing the inanimate body, with steady kicks of willpower, into imitation life.

Had I gone away, as I intended, I could have pre-served my reputation of pride and dignity: of the 'perfect Lady', their highest term of praise. Such a one, it can be imagined, stranded alone in a vanishing declivity in the hills among the God-forsaken estuary-haunted barbarians, does not have a large canvas of scope or opportunity, on which to spread herself. I wondered what she was supposed, but it was more a case of permitted, to do, according to their rigid dictates. A gentle spell of desultory gardening, inelegantly stooping in hand-woven tweed skirt, strung about with raffia baskets, chamois leather gloves and secateurs, vaguely weeding the herbaceous border, and clipping at random the rose beds. (Attacking a bed of nettles with a swiping scythe; rustily, bluntly pointing in every direction but the right one, slashing fearsomely at my ankles, at impeding tree trunks, at rebelliously rising fibrous roots, in a fury of lust to down the nettles in peril of death, was more my kind of penance of diversion.)

Or delicate water-colours of detailed split-in-half, botanical plants, or wishy-washy pale blue running waters with anaemic reflecting sunsets merging mauvely into them. And in the evening, whist drives; they could not afford tennis parties any more, and had stiff-jointedly outgrown them; with the last desert island survivals of decaying gentlewomen still tottering on their spindled herring-boned legs. There was the Women's Institute of course, but such a riotous participation entailed a distinct lowering in the social tone. She might even be so rustically adventurous as to 'indulge' in breeding better class poultry; but there is no avoiding that in the snob's hobby order of precedence, kennels are more *comme il faut* than hens, which, whichever way you don't look at them, are not quite *de rigueur*.

But, it was very odd, try as I would, I did not fit the role. There was something abnormally wrong with me. So instead I went to the opposite extreme, I did all the things a Lady should not do, and showed them, aggressively, just how unladylike a Lady can be. I gave myself up with selfless abandonment to being awful. I wallowed in excess; an excess of bodily surfeiting, to kill the critically carping maiden aunt of a mind that nagged the prostrate soul out of me. I sought filthily to purge the blood-thronging devils out of me by using the devil's own filthier-still instruments.

I stole their sons and husbands, doing violence to both our diversely raw feelings; violating purposefully my most precious holy vows to Dylan; saying his golden endearing words for me to them, making the same

18

familiar sweet affectionate gestures; ruthlessly pillaging the long years of our woven heart together; inciting a deliberate sacrilege, a shameful sacrifice of our love that was too stubborn to be put out. And all this fervour of destruction, to no, not one, flickering twinge of improvement, curative effect in my buried, unremitting black burning world; the ridiculous reverse: an increase in my inescapable dedication to Dylan and a mutilated guilt-soaked, pride-stripped body.

But the more they castigated, reviled and morally spat on me; they would gleefully have tarred and feathered me, and with screams of ecstasy, set light to me in the market square; the more I persisted in scandalizing them. Had they offered a grain of sympathy, a nod or a touch of understanding, it would have been my undoing: my tough, dissembling, distended-to-breaking-point guts, would have melted in a weak pool at their gracious feet. As it was, I managed to preserve, with admirable conviction; sometimes, I asked myself, was it true or was it not, because what one does with enough will, one may very well become; the impossible myth of the monstrous scarlet woman, till my eventual, bridge of wives, windily sighing with relief, departure.

'If only,' they whispered, and hissed in kitchen corners and back room bars malignantly, their bridling better-than-thou-ness glowing reassuringly in their wilting bird-caged breasts; '*she* could have waited a decent anonymity of years.'

Years; did you hear that; how much time do they think I have, and how do they propose that I should kill that deposited squeamishly out-of-sight shelf of years? If I waited a million years, I could not forget Dylan: he will not come blundering down the path again, all misshapen, bulgy lumpy shapes, his loaded head rolling with old unforgettable poems and growing miracles of to-

19

morrow singing, stifled, out of them; his pockets sagging with bottles and goodies, and bang at the door impatiently and shout, 'Cait, come down quick and let me in.' There will be nobody to bang at the door for he is in already.

But though I claimed to despise the morons, yet I minded terribly their unfriendliness, and was dying for a dram of kindness. I had given so much of myself to this God-forsaken, Dylan-shared, vanishing dip in the hills; much more than Dylan, who was so good at *containing* himself; that their turning on me and, metaphorically, stoning me out, made me feel like the most unjustly abused martyr.

The churchyard was always present to me, in that worst of awful periods, as an uncannily unbelievable place which, with all my elaborate deviations, I could never avoid landing up at; drawn by Dylan's rotting remains. And I would try to envisage how much was left of him; how much had started to crumble; and an impotent rage against the vile crudeness of nature daring to infringe on him, of all people, made me long to tear open that shoddy grey, speechless mound; ferret down to the long locked cold box, and burst it apart. There to press my headlong hot flesh into his, to mangle him with my strong bones, mingle, mutilate the two of us together, till the dead and the living would be desired One.

But instead I stood immovable, as near as possible without being seen, for I was ashamed to show myself in that conventional abode of lawful grief, and wept invisibly. And 'they' said: 'It is too much trouble for *her* to put a jampot of flowers on the grave.'

III

AND now I am on my way at last, in the Rome Express, with so much of Laugharne, the cemetery, and the whole of Dylan, good, bad, glorious, filling me, that I am impervious to chianti: though lapping it up as though parched in a desert for an eternity; vines, olives, and the extraordinary fact, that I am not treated as scum any more.

I thought it was not possible to feel any more: that I had gone to the dirty limits of my rat path; that having lost all I had, there was nothing left to lose; that I was immune, untouchable, inside and out, by anything that might conceivably happen to me. But I had not bargained for the rats following me quite so closely; for my weak vulnerability when faced with the screaming foreign world; for the innocent reproach of my bouncingly lively, too young son. How could the wretched worm know I was doing this absurd backward pilgrimage?— a thing I swore I was much too cynical to contemplate; where every landmark was as if I had seen it, and yet not seen it, before: that was the funny thing, that we never *saw*, noticeably, a single detached thing, so engrossed were we with our idiotic selves; and smote me with a new, old, faintly reminiscent thud. And the boy: I was either passionately kissing with guilt, furiously killing with irritation; or quietly cruising in some dim private region, out of reach of his relentlessly plebeian questions. And underneath all this play acting, though

21

I had washed my hands of God this long time, and was absolutely fed up with *His* cheating games, and underhand tricks on me, I kept saying: 'God, God, God.'

Whatever possessed me to think that a vague idealistic hunch, derived straight from my father's follies, would bring me sublime peace, and over the mountain fulfilment? When all that meets the eye on arrival is the ugliest town in the island, scarred on the coast with Nature's red brown gashes, from the steaming with chesty dust, iron mines. From the distance it is recognized by the permanent film of dust always resting above it. And we wondered why the place wasn't popular. Then the hypnotized staring when you venture out, making you feel like a blown-up deformity from the northernmost pole; which indeed, perhaps you think, you are. To make it more delectable still, I am put in *La stessa camera*, our old room, and I remembered every detail, since before Colm. There is an aspidistra pushed aside on the tiles, before-the-flood stag coat-hangers; and not an apology of hot water or bath to be had.

And the din; that is the best part to me, more the better, and less I understand the more sympathetic: from the clanging of the imperious church bells in the early morning, to the rising cackle of the market, right under our window, from seven onwards. By night time there is such a steady crescendo of piercingly conflicting sounds that to me it was as lullabying as the gentle lapping of waves; and the hotel is not even on the sea. In my turn, I could not help being amazed by the round plump bottoms precariously balanced on the long lean shanks; and topped by the soft, melting, seductive girl's film-star faces; these were the boys. And the men, the same thing hardened into sculptured shape; hewn hacked features, sun-drenched and toasted, and baked beautiful fiery black; and a lot of hair all over the place. And the women, mostly preserved in moth balls, and taken out for an airing once a year; more so than in Wales, if that is creditable. Only harridans visible roaring round the streets in wrinkled cotton stockings, rope shoes, and patched sackcloth.

I registered, with true distaste, that I still had the doubtful capacity for attracting the blackest, lowest, vermin among them, that obviously nobody else would dream of speaking to. They infallibly clustered and clung to me, like homing pigeons, alternatively sickening me with oily compliments or cheating me out of my few incomprehensible liras. Since I knew that all it took to exert this fatal fascination was an artificial blonde head, a pink, superficially baby—though let me reassure you quickly this was far from the case—face, and a body that bulged in and out, more or less, in the right places; I was not unduly flattered.

There was a man, when Dylan and I were here, who I thought possessed the ideal qualities: solidity, latent strength, tough as a rock, yet soft spoken, instinctively sensitive, and unembarrassed with learning; in short, the perfect leaning post. And a beauty of his own. I had saved up this man, The Church, for years, as something unique, an invaluable refuge, next to whom I could live happily for the rest of my years. So of course I was bound to prove this optimistic contention, with the easily conjecturable answer that, quite simply, his belly had got that much bigger, and his hair that much thinner; and those two insignificant trifles were sadly sufficient to break up the magic picture. He was as kind and good as ever, but leagues of country away, and once, as everybody knows, that unreasonable spell is broken, as soon flog a dead horse as try to revive it. However, he appeared satisfied with my dying-duck-in-a-thunderstorm airs and graces, and with no more palaver, gave me an unmistakable indication, with a fork over his shoulder, directed towards the bedroom door. Unaccountably this friendly invitation reduced me to a flood of tears again, as I contemplated how low was I fallen; and anxiously conjectured how much my compliance or refusal would affect the size of my bill. Still I held out with dolorous excuses, for the time being, and was grateful for Colm in my large bed.

With no exaggeration, the only respite in these first freezing, milestone days, was the hour when finally we were allowed to go to bed; and I could dive into my *Woman* and forget briefly where I was. How I dreaded finishing her. Like an over-hibernated squirrel, I went on distractedly chewing my nuts, and praying for one crack of spring; but none came. And my heart was strangling itself, in tightening knots, watching that child in a million; and that is not mother's milk talk, I promise, and can be corroborated by outsiders; Colm Thomas, lost, transplanted, his five years of magnified clarity in his tiny constricted puddle, pitted valiantly against the unspeakable barriers and horrors of the unknown. No language, no contact, but he is undeterred, uses all the wiles at his disposal, which are legion, and gets just where he wants to get: installed firmly, as the little favourite, deep in the sentimental Italian bosom. But this imitation tart's life, without the legitimacy of a man, is no good to him, or me.

Buckets of squalor and fecklessness: half the morning in and out of bed, all cluttered up with demolished trays of undrinkable tea, leaden bread, sour butter, and Colm's inevitable *aranciata*: fizzy orangeade: the only thing he would drink, except for beer; and spaghetti, the only thing he would eat, without fail at every meal, while pathetically pleading for his precious Weetabix; not exactly a balanced diet. Then a short stroll before lunch,

24

in a biting east wind, with Colm saying all the time: 'Come *on*, let's go home,' and as soon as I got back: 'Come *on*, let's go out,' not understanding that we had no home, and nowhere to go. After two days he was asking to go back to Laugharne; and how I sympathized! But what mother does not know the rock-bottom tyranny of these blackmailing cries; and is not torn asunder with loathing and love: with loathing well in the forefront. Till the object falls asleep *eventually*, like a conclave, a drove, an ecstasy of angels, and the mother: she has not got a hope in hell from the start; is overcome with guilt and remorse.

Anybody who thinks there is any vague chance of adult exchange with a child is up the spout; and would be much less disappointed if they recognized the chasm unbridgeably dividing, them. The cord that binds a mother to her child is not love in the sophisticated give and take sense: it is an organic, vegetable, all-giving function from the mother with no dotted-line returns, to which the child responds with the impersonality and egotism of a plant to the sun, as their natural and necessary birthright, in their smugly dominant kingdoms. So that if, at odd times, unsolicited, comes surprisingly an affectionate gesture, an amazing 'thank you', accept it serenely as a stray but exceptional dispensation, no more than that.

And so it goes on; and so it does for me; only I have no privacy in which to conduct these subterranean wars. I am constantly on parade, as bad almost as Royalty, minus their prestige and protection; so my first thought is a school for Colm, and that will be the devil's own to do; and a room for me, far away and alone, with radiogram, to practise my nonsense. It is hardly conceivable that I have not heard a single note of music, good or bad, and I do not mind which, so long as I hear it, as a breathing part of the day; that is to say pretty nearly all day long.

How I longed, and longed, and longed, for my incomparable sister Brigit, as I always did when I was in a really tight spot, and tried to imagine how she would have risen above this situation; because rise she would have, surely. She has that so rare universal quality, wonderfully devoid of pettiness or envy, yet never verging on sanctimoniousness; a vast acceptance and tolerance of every aberration of human nature. More than that, a spontaneous love and appreciation of people as themselves, of whatever class, or nationality; so naturally, as one, they worship this warming influence, and nobody wants to let her go.

I can see her now: large, awkward, clumsy, in shapeless clump coats, and clodhopping shoes, slung all over with shaming, misshapen bags and baskets; and a stream of actual, or imagined, both equally real at the power of her presence, children, begging and clinging after her. Rolling from side to side of the street, past the snake-bite vice of clamped men, apparently blissfully disregarding them. But she assured me, with rage afterwards, that this was not so, and she suffered far more than me, who, according to her, never showed a flicker of self-consciousness. Me, gazing rigidly into the far horizon, simulating an expression of disdainful superiority; pretending to be anybody but who I was: usually a tall, alabaster, voluptuously undulating creature, in a tight black velvet sheath, with slit tiger's eyes flashing. In total contrast to myself. And, in this guise, I did my utmost to convey that I was in no way, not in the smallest degree, related to that swashbuckling character, swaying by my side. So let there be no doubt as to my desirability; not I suppose that there was. So I asked myself now, a lifetime after, what would she have done in my place?

You can be sure she would not have sat, like the biggest fool on earth, in this same hotel bedroom, hesitating, pottering, wandering in and out, making tidying up motions, and answering her boy at random; till both of us were driven dippy. Not her—she would have been dressed, and on the go, since dawn, insisting on the right food for children, hustling them, taking them out for air (she had an indecent passion for air), whether they wanted it or not, making them feel they were something *worth* keeping alive. In no time we would be pleasantly organized, and there would be no yawning gaps in which to brood. With no more procrastination, I would gladly drop my niggling foibles and furbelows, and tag on to the fringe of her embracing train: my old impossible, frivolous self. It is a strain preserving this effigy of dignified, dutiful grief, that I have affected here; and in danger of becoming a permanent attire, unless I take myself with a smear of mustard. If I clowned till doomsday, that ghostly grief would still be riding high beside me. But Brigit would keep it at a presentable distance, with her no nonsense attitude, her concentration on essentials, immediate necessities: the bread and wine goodness underlying all my fancy prattling. She has the awesome gift of making you feel: and not only me to my chagrin; that she is the only person who understands the 'real' you, and knows how to bring out the best, deepest, richest deposits in you: need I say, a subject of unflagging, never dull for a second, unplumbable interest to *you*. But to save a constant hot bath of wallowing and self-indulgence, she has a blowing sense of outdoorness about her; never stops opening windows, metaphorical and otherwise, letting in remorseless cleansing winds; brushing away beloved cobwebs; and filling with healthy eating and clatter, the listening rooms. Then, without any warning, in the middle of a delicious revelation

27

perhaps, this paragon of a woman ups, and, with a curt, devastatingly casual Good-bye, goes. Simply disappears, and may not be seen again for a matter of years. And you feel alarmingly like a fledgling, chucked out of the nest unawares, and forced to use its own pitiable wings for the first time.

If ever a visitor was *not* charmed by the panorama, the throbbing colour (hadn't noticed either to tell the truth) and the artless, guileless, effervescing spirit of the island people, it is me: *not* charmed. It is hard to know whether to despise or admire, that childish arrogance and ease of movement, that leisurely *laisser aller*, that concerns itself only with itself; it is impossible not to envy it. And those proud young women in skin-tight skirts, undeniably glued on to the eloquent thighs and hips; three inch heels; glossy raven hair; walking an interminable dusty road, with nobody but the crone-straddled asses to admire them. Except me, that is.

One formidable step I at last took, with agonized pushing and trepidation; sent Colm to school. Had I sent him to the guillotine, I couldn't have suffered more: but, after a lot of fuss, terror at them staring at him, he had felt it too, talking gibberish to him, and fantastic bribes on my part: I got him there. It was not quite so torturous as I feared: a darling smiling Sister, I was converted there and then; and a row of dazzling, ribbon-crisp, spick and span, pink check-pinafored small boys. Instead of leaving Colm, hanging about disconsolately in the background, as though he were nothing to do with *them*, as they mostly do in my experience, my beautiful Sister took him by the hand, led him to the front of the class, and presented him by name, explaining that he was English, and asking them to be nice to him.

He was received with cries of joy and clapping, and I could see that his reception pleased him immensely. I sent up a silent prayer of gratitude, and crept back, still screwed up in knots of tension, to sit among the debris of the night.

I should be in the fields, six hours a day, doing sweated labour; before I could sort myself out. I would willingly, but I do not seem to have the nerve to, any more, make myself an obvious freak (I am accustomed to the crank inside me, and try to camouflage it); and I do not think I could stand, just now, the open mouthed comments, the shrill exclamations!

But my school troubles were not over, of course: the second day is nearly always more difficult, because they think they have done it, once and for all, and it is all over. So when you cajolingly suggest taking them back again the next day, then they dig the heels of rebellion in, hard and sharp, with the double weapon of tears, and there is a good old-fashioned mother and son outburst. If the mother wins this round, she is entitled to feel comparatively safe. He was worried by the prodding, and poking, and avid questioning of older girls: as if he was a fascinatingly foreign pet monkey; and I sympathized, after Wales, from the bottom of my heart. Nevertheless, I tried to reassure myself, I, and *the* bedroom, were infinitely worse for him. And for once I was not being selfish; well not entirely. And the vision of him, in one of those always coveted, utterly disarming pinafores, hands folded, with the rest, in prayer, heads bowed, shrill voices babbling, was much too touching for even my bashed heart to resist.

And so the monotonous piling up of the hours goes on: is it scientifically tenable that we have not yet been a week on this ugly chunk of rock? I, for one, am very sceptical. The clever procedure in a new, and especially as strange a place as this, is to lie low and bide your time, masticating more than you expectorate. Till you are, if not as canny as your protagonist—that would be over optimistic for anybody, let alone me, to aspire to; in possession of a measure of confidence, in possession of yourself is what it amounts to; and able to discriminate roughly between the sheep and the lambs, the wolves, the swan, and the ugly duckling.

The Church would sometimes take us on his mock motor bike; the island is swarming with these perfect comical toys, and I should love to have one myself, to disappear with, if they didn't gaze so blatantly; Colm, Colombo as they call him, standing in front, bulky man planted in middle, and me perched, skirts, bags, and hair flying in all directions, behind; to cruise along the coast, on corkscrew death-trap roads, or climb the precipitous savage mountains. I was blankly immune to the imitation Old Master landscape, and nervously working out how much fear I should femininely show; and the corresponding degree of correct clutching, round the immovable backside of The Church, overshadowing me. I had been perhaps too precipitate in my first repulsive action; and was a little piqued that he did not persevere. There are times when good manners and consideration are out of place, and a 'won't-have-no-for-an-answer' insistence would be more flattering. Not that I wanted him, *far* from it.

But he was so good, it made me want to cry, and he didn't even know it. It stuck out, in great beams, with every step he took, every action he made, every word he said. How could such a log of goodness be let loose among the schemers and parasites, and still keep his oaken integrity unmolested? But nobody seemed to notice anything out of the ordinary about him; I suspect he must have had a shrewd Italian side I knew nothing about: he was, after all, a good business man, and a capitalist for the island. But if I didn't know much about him, he certainly knew *nothing* about me, beyond the flimsy externals, which, I suppose, is just as well. Our conversations were confined to monosyllabic '*Questo bello*'s, so not much headway could be made in that direction: and there is nothing more irritating than not to have, at your disposal, the words you want.

IV

DYLAN was always about three jumps ahead of me, and
had already put the argument backwards, inside out, and
upside down, by the time I had got it eventually standing
up straight. And this trick of always demolishing, with
the invaluable aid of ridicule, a perfectly adequate work,
or, just as soon, a masterpiece, then rebuilding it in his
own freakish fashion, used to make me hopping cross;
presumably because I was out of my depths. And he
insisted, though I never agreed, that women have *no*
sense of fun: verbal fun I think he meant; and were a
spewing mass of generalizations and clicks (as our high-
brow poetess in Laugharne calls clichés), only fit for the
bed and the kitchen.

When I wake in the morning, when it is still dark, before even the bells or hullabaloo below has started, with
the tears streaming, uncalled for, down my face, and
Colm sleeping so small and reminiscently against me; and
remember who I am, and where I am, and think of
Dylan: Dylan in Laugharne, Dylan in this island, and
Dylan wherever I am; and pine, as keenly as a sick cow
for its calf just removed, for the feel of him, the smell of
him; and go on daftly half waiting for him to come back,
when I know he cannot; but it is not a bit of good for
reason to tell me that, it cannot stop the wanting so
badly, reasonable or not; and where can I put it, what
can I do with it? It is not a chasm, it is an enormous
fruit cake, of wanting: I am invaded with a stream of

32

incessant babbling, jingly, jangling; oh, why can't it stop for a minute? yesterdays. And the tomorrows stretch in somnolent torpor, paying no attention to my gnawing and prodding behind the shutters.

I go to the glass, look into the pin-pointed, criss-crossed holes which contain, a thousand fathoms back, my ensnared reproachful eyes; and think, 'This is not the Rock Caitlin that Dylan loved: this damp, bedraggled string of seaweed.' And he would flood me with a contempt of words; there is no fury like the weak, against the weak; and he knew how to use words insultingly, as well as poetically. But because of his own Welsh hypochondrias he hated to see any sign of them in others and had no patience with any nervous ailments or manifestations in his children, because they came from him; though prepared to nurse his own, or preferably be nursed if that were forthcoming, with loving care, and wealth of descriptive detail.

He was never his proper self till there was something wrong with him; and, if ever there was a danger of him becoming 'whole', which was very remote, he would crack another of his chicken bones, without delay, and wander happily round in his sling, piling up plates with cucumber, pickled onions, tins of cod's roe, boiled sweets; to push into his mouth with an unseeing hand, as they came, while he went on solidly reading his trash. His passion for lies was congenital: more a practice in invention than a lie. He would tell quite unnecessary ones, which did not in any way improve his situation: such as, when he had been to one cinema, saying it was another, and making up the film that was on: and the obvious ones, that only his mother pretended not to see through, like being carted off the bus into his home, and saying he had been having coffee, in a café, with a friend.

The reason we got along so well in the house was because of our mutually organic—meaning the organs were functioning but not much else—natures when off parade. The home was to Dylan, more especially, a private sanctum, where for once he was not compelled, by himself admittedly, to put on an act, to be amusing, to perpetuate the myth of the *Enfant Terrible*: one of the most damaging myths, and a curse to grow out of. We lived almost separate lives, though physically close, and passed each other with a detached phrase on strictly practical matters; as though we were no more than familiar landmarks, in the furniture of our minds. Excluding the times, more frequent at night, when the house rattled, and banged, and thudded, and groaned with our murder of each other.

But these fights, which were an essential part of our everyday life, and became fiercer and more deadly at each onslaught, so that you could have sworn no two people reviled each other more; and could never, under any fabulous change of circumstances, come together again: were almost worth-while because, when the reconciliation did take place, according to how long we could stick it out, it was so doubly, trebly, quadruply sweet, and we could never have ventured to conceive of such a thing happening again.

As far as the waiting game was concerned, I was the millimetre of an inch more adept than Dylan: owing to more false pride, and, as I sadly see now, more time to play around, so that it was he who nearly always made the first move back to normality, while I was reluctantly persuaded. And thinking back now, I see he was in a great hurry to fit in so many things; and could not be bothered with the extra spade work that to most people is compulsory. And many afternoons he wanted me to go to bed with him, and I would not because of some

34

ridiculous Upright principle that I chose to presume guided me. (God has some queer twists up His sleeve and, by whatever means you try to outwit or anticipate Him, He will nip you just where you least expect it.)

Jesus, he even kept saying he would die before me: would never reach forty: and I would be a flighty widow dancing on his grave. And I laughed, completely unmoved; for all the impression it made on me, he might as well have been talking to an elephant. And other things, to my discredit, come back to me: how he used to pursue me with the latest version of a poem in progress; and only ask me to stand still and let him read it to me; and how I would wriggle, do everything in my power to escape, block my ears (I hope without showing it), till in the end, he could not but notice my surly unwillingness, and swore never to read to me again, but always did. And this behaviour I find plain unforgivable, no two ways about it, and I can't account for my reaction, because I always had faith in Dylan as a poet: and even helped over choosing alternative words and on small points of preference; and he had a touching belief in my judgment. Putting it on the kindest level, I can say, I must have subconsciously felt I had something of my own worth preserving, and did not want to be influenced by Dylan's highly disturbing stuff. On the unkindest: that I was spitefully jealous, and resented, like any typical, man-swallowing woman, such a powerful rival to myself. But this I will not, and do not believe, even now. And I did all I could to make him work, at his own special work, and not public money-making work. And it was only with our kind of purely vegetable background, which entailed months on end of isolated, stodgy dullness and drudgery for me, that he was flattened out enough to be able to concentrate.

One of the most remarkable things about him, to me,

35

was his singular gift for adapting himself to every kind of different, basically opposed, person and place. With no visible transition he would settle down among the new set, as though he had been there all his life. And with equal ease cut off the old like dead leaves: though retaining surprising loyalties to old buddies, and motherly bodies overlapping and spilling with fistfuls of fat: one of our favourite kill-times in Laugharne was to sit in the window of the Brown's, and imagine these Colossi (with which Laugharne was well stocked) walking, ten abreast, up the street, stark naked. And calculate how much money we would give to see such an impressive sight: nearly all we had.

So he was much better than me at contenting himself with the very simple, I might justly say moronic, life. Because, there is no other possible explanation, he lived in a world of his own: 'out of this world', as they so succinctly put it in America. Thus: the best part of the morning in the kitchen of this same high class establishment, putting bets on horses, listening, yes, actually listening for once, open mouthed, to local gossip and scandal, while drinking slow consecutive pints of disgustingly flat, cold-tea, bitter beer. Muzzily back to late lunch, of one of our rich fatty brews, always eaten alone, apart from the children; and I can't blame him for that, as there is nothing worse than brawling children's meals. He went so far, like a respectable Victorian father, as not travelling in the same carriage with them, though it was not often we went anywhere *en masse*, and I cannot blame him for that either. Then, blown up with muck and somnolence, up to his humble shed, nesting high above the estuary; and bang into intensive scribbling, muttering, whispering, intoning, bellowing and juggling of words; till seven o'clock prompt.

Then straight back to one of the alternative dumps:

we had long discussions as to which was the deadliest; to spend the rest of the evening in 'brilliant repartee'. That was a sample day with all the innards and lights taken out.

V

BACK to the bloody island, and the back-breaking of it.
That I had not yet had a bath, in over a week, and must
have been stinking to high heaven; plus the end of the
month embarrassments, which make a point, especially
abroad, of catching me unprepared, and consequently
saddling me with the most medieval contraptions, had
not helped to lift my morale. And though these may
seem small things to the uninitiated, the initiated will
fully sympathize.

The only advantage to be gleaned from this state of
siege was that it kept The Church at a cool distance,
though as I indicated, he was a shade too ready to be
cooled off. I wanted to make a friendly gesture towards
him, that would not be interpreted as an invitation, but
without appropriate words, and the patting motion only
pleasing to a dog: it was very difficult. So I contented
myself with squeezing him from the back of his motor
bike, where I felt strategically placed. He had a son
about to be married, soft, smiling, with already thinning
hair, who bore out my contention of the fathers being so
much more attractive than their sons. Beside his father
the son was non-existent; and gradually I was beginning
to grasp, over the seven-year boulder of contradictory
experience, the built-up, from one root dug in its native
soil, cored power of the man.

And my body, which at home I treated with some
respect, pummelling and pounding, and chivvying it into

shape and tingling awareness of itself; shifting the sluggish blood; had never lain so long inactive: a stunted drugged tape worm, without the gumption to uncoil itself. And as my mental armoury—a couple of worn-out pea-shooters—responded in exact ratio to my physical condition, try to visualize the atrophied knots clogging my poor wilting senses.

But I must try to enumerate the drops of healing ointment in this ocean of complaint: the search for a place to sit down, unobserved, rewarded. After assiduous dodging of the all-seeing eyes, I discovered, up some viney henpecked terraces behind the town, a single, leafy, concealing tree, which, when I looked up, I saw to be covered with my favourite, packed with fertility, figs. Although the ground was dry and stony and tufted with coarse grass, I could crouch underneath blessedly almost invisible. Two: going to fetch Colm from school, and hearing, from right down the street, Colm roaring with laughter; when I asked him casually what it was about, he said the Sister had been telling them stories about putting rats and spiders down people's clothes. I know he has a great power of invention, like somebody else, but even so. I crossed myself and left it at that. It was disconcerting the amount of friends he had, not among children of his own age, but with the best looking lads of the town. They would spend hours fooling around with him, and trundling him up and down on bicycles; so that he was naturally crazy about them, and discipline was a dead loss. He would say grandly: 'My friends are waiting.' And they genuinely were, as keen as he was.

And the third miracle: that I had actually touched water at last; the real, clean, buoyant Mediterranean. Disregarding temporarily the perpetual red dust bath that pervaded and coloured everything: Colm was plastered from head to foot by the end of the day, the sea was stained burnt sienna for yards out, and the beaches, which were nearly all rocks, were black with starry sediment. I still find it hard to credit that we hardly noticed it before, and would exclaim with surprise, 'How lucky that this place is not popular.' It would be very odd if it were, when out of all the romantic towns, and snow-white beaches, with sand like large granulated sugar, this is the only mining shanty town on the island, which has the one grace of saving it from the shanty appurtenances of a resort. And the sun is out in October; a sun that it is possible to lie in comfortably without scorching; though, even so, a bit too much for Colm with the long mine-laboured trek; and the full summer would definitely have killed him; so I thought, with my first satisfaction, perhaps my timing was not so bad after all.

And I determined, if I could, by a carefully devised method, and strict monastic routine, somehow endure the coming months, I would stay on over Christmas, and the next three sure killer ones, till April—when Wales begins to stir again. Otherwise all this effort and pain of initiation would be wasted, and no benefit derived for either of us. And I did want us at least to master the colloquialisms of the language, and to feel a part of, and not a visitor to, the country. As it was, I was the only person without a function, with no set work to do: just the English widow on holiday, to recover from her sorrow; no more ignominious role; there must be *something* more for me to do.

Not a note of music, not a line of reading matter; no distraction of any kind, apart from weather, and food, which had developed into a nun's orgy; and animated actors on a garish, but scantily convincing cardboard stage. And most of all I missed the music, to push away, put into perspective, this harsh, jarring, too representative reality. One engulfing pull, breast-filling draught, from that bespectacled midget Casals, on his great, planet-encompassing 'cello, and this little township would fade into its proper place in the background of respectful attention. Or a spine-curdling aria from Gigli, to make them sit up and forget the price of fish, if only for the inspired length of that voice: where are the procreators of all these famous tenors we hear so much about?

And so to the rats: with my unerring flair I had lured, not with my co-operation, the biggest rat in the business to my defenceless side. There is one in every town, and this one put me in mind of a similar one, who used to scratch and scrape, and sniff and twitch his ugly whiskers at us, in the Chelsea gutter days. They always look like hamming stage villains with moustaches—was there ever a clean-shaved ratman?—pulled-down slouch hats, and slinky shiny clothes, especially the shoes, with points. And they have a glib, soft-soap line of patter. And the local one was no exception: and he rode on a Vespa, which also was in keeping. Finally, after evading his pressing invitations for as long as was decently polite, and being warned by The Church to have nothing to do with him, I succumbed, and handed him the body and soul of Colm and me, to drive to rat damnation. And what a skinny twisted back he had, after the comforting bulk of The Church; I was beset with fears and doubts: that to punish me, Colm would be hurled down a precipice: and that, I decided, would fix me: the knife would go in, up to the hilt, this time, no messing. But, as is often disappointingly the case, there was a sucking babe inside this vermin skin of wickedness.

However, his first concern was to find out, by not very subtle means, in fact by asking point blank, what was my age, and how much money had I got. But I can act dumb too, on occasion, and the lack of language could here be used to my advantage. Then that most putting off of all tricks, the producing of written credentials: a sure sign of a suspicious louse of the lowest order. A little later, as we walked in the desolate pinewoods, on the bleak white sands, he made a few dutiful unimpassioned passes at me; but his performance was not brilliant and hardly capable of deceiving a maiden aunt. So, damped in his heavy going ardours, he did a neat lightning switch over to more mundane immediacies, and, rather late in the day, suggested a drink, which did us both a lot more good.

(We had suffered before from this unwelcoming Italian habit. When they got you, never again after the first couple of times, into their houses: cool, shaded, bare but for a few flimsy pieces of polished wood, skidding on stone floors; and bereft of the merest rug of human contamination: they sat you down, with much ceremony, and you politely waited, with an occasional glance at the array of bottles of different wines on the sideboard; but no offers were forthcoming; and the conversation would steadily become more stilted. With Dylan it would have been different: he would have had the uppishest dowager duchess herself relating her sex life with gusto; and have insisted on constant supplies of beer for himself, regardless of anybody else, including me.)

So we set out and he went on and on, a long, long way: I thought he would never stop, and we would never see the, now metropolitan, lights of Rio again. We landed on Campo, which had everything that Rio had not, including sun-glassed, time-tabled, bronzed, exuding, even in their exclusive briefs, their superior status, Americans; French; Germans; and a singular soullessness. So my immediate wish was 'home', as fast as possible. Is it true

42

I am calling Rio 'home'? So without too much persuasion of the now slightly flagging rat, we remounted the jolting Vespa, and started the cold and windy return journey. We wedged Colm between us for warmth, and the wretched rat was pushed precariously on to the handle bars; I felt sure the judgment was upon us now, with Colm dropping off to sleep, his survival depending solely on the strength of my arm. But, with a couple of stops for marsala and cognac, and tea for Colm, which put a dream hazy complexion on the tawdry and dangerous proceedings, we made it. Then he did his final act of rattishness: dumped us outside the town to avoid people talking, not for my sake, but for his. And left in a great hurry, as though he had never seen us before.

When we eventually trailed back, worn out, to the hotel, the whole family was standing in united disapprobation at the top of the stairs. The Church would not say a word to me, and my exhausted nerves began to inexcusably giggle, of all schoolgirl shames. But really he was impossible, this man, ruffling himself up like a turkey cock, and putting on such ridiculous airs of proprietary indignation; it had obviously never crossed his mind, not once in his life, that he himself might be wrong: such a fabulous contingency was against the law of the island. I felt for him in return, in exact proportions—disgust, shyness, old attraction seeping through, and fresh admiration for his cavalier treatment of me; it is a sad facet of human nature that we respect most those who spit on us. As for shyness I thought I had long ago done away with that bogey—that British excuse for churlishness, awkwardness, and downright rudeness; but I felt coming back, in this sensually polished environment, all the rawness, and cruel crudities: pent up silences, of that unenviable adolescence.

Then I met the only Englishman on the island, married

to an Italian woman, and he had that hunted, come-to-the-end-of-his-tether look; he told me, with a yearning, shining light in his moist eyes, he was due to get out, to the home country, at the end of the month. And he was strongly anti-English, considered gone irretrievably native; but ominously hounded by the dogged traditions. He drank in the strictly miserable, continuous, solemn duty, British style, quietly packing it away, and getting steadily more taciturn. However, he was not proof against the Englishman's (or American's, for that matter) vice: before I left, out came the ponderous portfolio, packed to bursting point, with closely written pages of thin paper: his handiwork. And would I just open it anywhere, and give a cursory opinion on the style and construction, and a spot of advice on his story: war experiences, needless to say: 'knocked out at odd moments'. How was I going to get out of this one? Off I went, nursing the awkward bundle, and deposited it tenderly at the bottom of my trunk, for future courage.

Whenever I met the Englishman, though we were the last people in England to have anything in common—he was a public-schooled, at least he acted like one, mason: my two pet aversions—we fell upon each other, not physically, but verbally, and started gabbling like the two sole survivors on a sinking ship. He poured out the intimacies of his married life, which, by the cut-throat tension that reared itself around them, when they were together, I gathered had reached that stage, when whatever the other one said, or did, was a personal affront.

He was the only person who appeared to have as little reason to be on the island as me; his whole day was spent sitting on the end of a ramshackle wooden breakwater, or pier, on a camp stool, with burberry and check cap, holding a bent, defeated fishing line, by the patient hour. I never saw him land a fish, but he had been known to get two or three very occasionally. Or, as a revolutionary change in the seven-year routine: yes, he had weathered seven years in this barracks, and hark at me talking after a bare century of two weeks; he would plant himself on one of the old tug boats in the harbour; and to show how far gone I was, I would plant myself alongside, to watch him waiting, waiting, waiting, for that magical twitch that never came.

He had an ingrown Scotch-biassed prejudice: than which there is nothing more obstinate, against the Italians, and when I asked him what it was that offended him most in them, he said, with no hesitation, with clipped martial condemnation: 'Unreliability.' And when I mildly pointed out that it was not such a terrible crime after all, I could see the temper diffusing through his briary body, to crackle in his bloodshot eyes; then he turned on me in fury barking; I had never heard a man bark before, but the magazines are right again, they can: that it was the *only* thing that mattered; that he had not asked me for my opinion anyhow; there were certain things that were better not discussed; and what is more, did I realize, they only shaved three times a week! When I did not blanch in horror at this shocking revelation, but said I found the American obsession for hygiene more indecent: constantly rubbing away the original sin—he went on, utterly ignoring me, enumerating the Italian filth, explaining, as to the innocent among thieves, that there were certain people one could speak to, and certain people that one could not, and it simply was not done for people, like us, to have anything to do with them; there were only three people in Rio, he said, that he spoke to, and they were not his class. He indicated the man sitting beside me and announced

45

pompously: 'It might interest you to know that you are drinking with the local dustman; and I for one would prefer not to be in his company.' I could not help laughing at this, and calling him a fascinating old-fashioned snob, while explaining, in my turn, that snobbery was the other way round these days, and his was out of date. This clinched the acrimonious discussion, and he rose up, and stalked out of the café, in shaking indignation. So my last link with dubious civilization vanished, not a tragedy in itself, but I felt some regret at my access to the tug boat, and fish vigils, being taken away.

So I was left to the tedious mercies of the maligned dustman: truthfully he was getting on my nerves too, though for different reasons: he was one of those unfortunates who had been to America, had a pretty tough time, probably done every kind of sweated labour, reserved for down and outs, and made a big story out of it, which he would never live down. So he insisted on talking to me, his bastard pidgin-English: when I was dying to talk to him, my bastard pidgin-Italian: the result, in either case, was beatified incomprehension. So, although he was a poor old sod, with a broken comb-toothed mouth, dark glasses, and clothes which, it was evident, had never been put on, and off: but had taken root, in the barren soil, and were growing on him; or *because* he was such a one, it was now a question of *my* principles, and a point of honour, though I was just on the point of discarding him, that I should follow him to the ends of the earth.

The function of the dustman, as I had observed it, was to bicycle round the streets, propelling a wooden box on wheels, in front: and, into this receptacle, to dump with elaborate ramifications, and to the slow voluptuous, hip-swaying rhythm—which, whether they were serving at table, or pickaxeing into the adamant granite of the

46

mountains, they could no more accelerate than a cat can get its fur wet (they shared the same abhorrence of water too)—the stinking refuse, of animal remains and excesses that daily cluttered the streets. Then they drove the heaped-up load to the edge of the cliff, tipped it carelessly half over, in a high wind, and the whole lot promptly blew back into the town. Soiled papers and rags flew up to the ever open, grandstand windows, with women, and lines of washing, permanently fluttering out of them.

I began to see why no other distraction was necessary: window gazing, from inwards, downwards, not outward, was as serious an occupation as any, and went on from early morning, in relays through the day, to nightfall. And I found myself cultivating the habit without thinking. And the performers on the street below, conscious of their audience, excelled themselves in the fervour of their buying and selling.

And glimpsed rarely, neatly descending the centre steps, carrying vast tubs of washing on their heads, without using hands, balanced on a circular pad thing; the wives, and daughters. The daughters with profuse, spreading, flowering bushes of hair: waving lions' manes, jet-black plaited horses' tails; hair that leads a life of its own, that must be constantly held in check, fenced in, tamed, for fear it run riot, and despoil the face of womanhood. Even now trickling darkly down the gorilla legs. Then those bodies with the one-purpose only look: it seems a waste of time to dress them, as they look more undressed dressed, than were they prim naked; and they make of Renoir's insipid, faded beauties, a gathering of British matrons, at an afternoon garden fête. Whereas in Wales I always felt out of place, with too many bright colours regardlessly clashing together, here I was a dowdy, wispy, strait-laced school teacher, rapidly blowing up, on rich food and unlimited wine, into a blowsy Rubens.

But bulges or no bulges, and these were no romantic curves; as my dear mother would sweetly say, when I had swathed myself in flowing draperies to simulate the Queen of Sheba: 'Very nice, dear, but you are not quite the type; all our family are *stubby*.' *Stubby*: if ever there was a word to damp the romantic cravings in a girl; I was now faced with the terrible decision to be put in writing right away, am I to go back for Christmas, well over a month away, or am I to commit myself to eternal purgatory in this hole: bearing in mind that the other side was a hole of purgatory too. The question to decide was: which one would be the more depressing: not a very invigorating choice; not forgetting my rule, very imperfectly followed lately, never to go backwards, into the unrevivable past; but always be ready to clasp the impending disasters. One thing I have irrefutably proved, that however immune you may think yourself to be, to the bag of tricks in store, you need not worry, *He* will get at you, through some faultily cemented crevasse, and twist the needle. And consider, this is the life of leisured freedom, that most people dream about! and I did too. Little they know the burden of decision, the apportioning of the hours to unnecessary tasks, which I do my best to pretend are necessary, knowing all the time that whether they are done or not, makes no difference to man or beast. That hill that has *got* to be climbed; that path that it is essential to follow. Do but give me some plain-sailing oakum to pick; I don't know what it is, but I should love to pick it; and a vicious slavedriver at my back to whip me on; that would be, as Colm says, 'poppish': a derivation of 'easy as pop'; compared to my hithering, thithering, not knowing whithering, floating bloating, waste of saturation.

Then I could wholeheartedly revile my fate, and say I was meant for better things. But now that I have got better things, and only myself to revile, what do I do but complain about my lack of chains, and go searching, and screeching, and banging into walls, like a blinded demented hen, looking for a master to tell me what to do, and when; so that, presumably, I shall have the pleasure of doing the opposite again. For that is another of those little bittersweet ironies, that wrongdoing loses its savour when it is made permissible; and only the unprocurable is a luxury. So now that nobody cared what I did, nor tried to stop my exaggerated exhibitions of myself, just to *show* I was afraid of nothing, the bite was deftly taken out of the apple. And replaced by a quaking aspen leaf, that was me, not sure of which foot to put in front of the other, in which direction to turn my eyes, stumbling, belatedly newly born, wandering, bereft, in a dense country of confused woods, stifled by too many trees. Where no door was open to me, and I was always the interloper on the threshold. Always on the outside looking in: desperately envying the belonging people, avidly watching the positive domestic moves; the cascading revelation of soap suds, the regimented, wind-grained linen wound on to the ceiling, the miracle of sweet-smelling, hot-lamb's-wool, crusted bread; as though I had never seen, or touched, these dream images before.

I saw a funeral, which reminded me, no, not of Dylan's for God's bloody sake, of one we had seen together before in Rio; which, even then, had made an impact on me, though I was not ready for it, and did not know where it hit me. This one did the same, and I still don't know where it hit me; but it was all so carefully, yet beautifully casually, worked out: without a loophole for the human emotions to get out of hand: a continual litany of chant, to cover up the unseemly disorders of grief. And the chief mourners, why are they invariably women, wedged tight between the nearest relatives, with a rearguard, in block formation, of dependants, following up behind. And the vulgar emblems of tinnily entwined paper flowers carried aloft; and the priest in front murmuring everyday Latin endearments to his cross; and in the midst, but 'set' a few paces apart, as though the people were afraid to get too close, the small, ornate, locked fast, box, with gargantuan brass handles, swaying perilously, on the shoulders of the closest, down-faced friends. And the dust coming, the wind ruffling the high-pitched crowd, the sea blaring unheard below. And the regular catholic voices beating and beseeching; trained to constrain the wild terror in the heart of each of them.

Then I couldn't help thinking of Dylan's too, and contrasting that tame, cup of tea, whisky-nipping, saucepan-domesticated, mingling of the original black beetles, raffish Londoners, and Swansea boys in their best provincial suits. And all caring according to their means, and class. But caring, more than anybody had cared at a funeral since: but I am afraid it is impossible for me to think of anybody who could have been so cared for. And had there been no caring, I could have done it all, alone. And 'After the funeral, mule praises, brays. . . .'

And then it started to rain; here, when it was wet, it still looked dry, from months on end of sucking up sun; but there, in the Welsh bogs, when it was sunny, although never without an alleviating cloud, it still looked wet. And the earth was deliciously damp, grassy and vaporous; and though I wouldn't say so, how much I wanted it. How much I wanted so many things I couldn't give a name to. So many things which disowned me, but still stuck in me. Then I thought of the awful things too, that I had left behind me: the extremely drab; between which and the heroic, the one a product of the other, an inseparable gulf of bourgeoisie simmered. And, although I realized this bug was as rampant here as anywhere, if not more so, it was kept more out of sight, incarcerated in black, holy family, corsets.

VI

I AM not, to my unlimited sorrow, a spontaneous person;
not since my halcyon Isadora Duncan days, when I
chose to fancy myself as flowing with melody, movement,
and everything but the kitchen sink, including Grecian
draperies, and Mercurian sandals, no half measures for
me. It did not occur to me that all that flows is not, of
necessity, gold; was it not *me* who was flowing? As a
matter of fact it was not; being me, I was tying myself in
knots, and refusing to respond to the music, though I
could hear, quite distinctly, what it was saying to me;
and one hitch of the brain too late, would spring into
action. Whenever I did come, triumphantly one with the
music: I am not using the expression 'come' loosely, I
mean in the loving sense; no loving come ever gave such
prolonged ecstasy. And I did, comparatively often when
I was alone; but as soon as I spotted the 'glance' of an
audience, I was finished: the brain on the alert, all
suspicion again, put the pincers on, and the capricious
flow stopped abruptly. I was as lost as a sleepwalker,
tapped unawares into wakefulness on the edge of a roof,
and had no more idea where I was or what to do next:
the music was a meaningless noise offending my ears,
and obstructing my thinking.

This was one reason, now I come to think of it, why
Dylan found it so annoying: it is the direct opposite of
words, and talk; and, in a greater, and deeper degree, of
poetry. It may be one of the substances that poetry is

made out of; that words are formed from; but its elemental—right back, through the encumbering ages, to the creation, the planets, the floods, the dinosaurs; the skeletons and protoplasm—force is, above any other point of supremacy, *wordless*. So that to pin it on to poetry, as an accompaniment, is not only an absurdity, but an insult to both. How Dylan would have loathed this style of abstract ranting, as he would have called it, of mine; but I should never have dared put it down if he was going to see it.

He had the same dislike, amounting to superstitious horror, of philosophy, psychology, analysis, criticism; all those vaguely termed ponderous tomes; but most of all, of the gentle art of discussing poetry; not that I was likely to do that. We had a mutual agreement to keep off that touchy subject; and, if well-meaning friends started an abstruse, intense interpretation of some of Dylan's most obscure lines, which he had long ago forgotten the meaning of himself, it was not long before Dylan was on the floor wrapped up in the carpet, scratching himself, like a flea-bitten hyena, in paroxysms of acute boredom, ending, happily for him, in snoring amnesia. Not that such a delicate hint deterred the everlasting friend, who had now, by devious, unrelenting routes, introduced his own verse; and a dash of existentialism as well; while I was left politely nodding over the soup, planning all the hells I would put Dylan through for this, and wishing I had not been so well brought up; never to speed the parting guest; who, it was evident, had no intention of departing.

This very pronounced attitude of Dylan's against every type of flowery excursion into intellectualism made all the more surprising his extreme patience and tolerance in America, when confronted with the full blast of their adulation. There is, it appears, no limit to the quantity of flattery that one person is prepared to take about themselves; and, from whatever source, and, however far-fetched, they show a remarkable indulgence on this, their pet topic. I am perfectly alive, from my own vain experience, to the large part vanity plays in the least suspected lives: quite apart from our shameless flamboyancy. But Dylan always seemed to me to stand right outside this poetical junketing, this clannish backbiting, these teaspoon-tongued, little-finger-extended, oh so too too, Societies for the Prevention of Cruelty to Poets; if for the only reason that he had no need to swim in those shallow babbling waters. So that when he succumbed, like a mesmerized bait, only in this case a short-legged one, to the multitudinous, scavenging, spawn of America, I knew, though I was too falsely proud to let myself know, it was the end of me; and, not long after, the fatal end of him.

It is easy to understand that, when the unflagging, disarming American charm met Dylan's professional charm, it caused a general melting fudge of a sticky, syrupy, irresistible fluid, impossible for such as us: raw from the harsh Welsh backward blacknesses, starved of any public attention; accustomed to the half-said, half-swallowed greeting; the ever-present fear of a taint of effusion; both incapable of saying *No* to any invitation, in case we missed something: to extricate ourselves from, intact. Because it got me, at second hand, as a thankless extension of Dylan, and even then, from that comparatively safe distance, barbed and horned as I was, it was too much for me, and I was left a soulless lump of inanimate meat. So what can Dylan have felt like, in spite of his incredible resistance, and amazingly quick recovery powers? One moment he was flat out, in utter self-abandonment, coughing and heaving up his heart, down to the soles of his boots; the next, dolled up, like a puppy's supper, dapper and spruce, or as near as he could get to it. But there was always a grotesque flaw in the tailor's dummy, which, if I mentioned, I was slaughtered; and if I did not I was blamed for not being interested. Jocularly joking, as though that other prostrate negation, parody of a romantic poet in tubercular convulsions, had no connection in the narrow world, with him. Then nervously twitching, and acrimoniously nagging me, about tiny petty things, which neither of us took seriously; but which outsiders were alarmed into thinking was at least the breaking up of our marriage. But our marriage was not a cobweb house drifting on sand; and we enjoyed the back chat, if nobody else did.

So, with the last burning question: 'Was he better with a hat on or off?' to which I always answered: on; but that did not please him either, because he thought I meant there would be less of him to see. The momentous decision between a bow tie and a long one, with the spotted bow a certain winner; and between two equally dirty, scrofulous pairs of trousers, that had stood, all night, in concertina'd neatness, at the foot of the bed; he was off to the Killer, poetry reading.

Dylan used to read to me in bed, in our first, know-nothing, lamb-sappy days; to be more exact, Dylan may have been a skinny, springy lambkin, but I was more like its buxom mother then, and distinctly recollect carrying him across streams under one arm; till the roles were reversed, and he blew out, and I caved in, through the pressure of family life, and the advent of holy-fire destroying babies. He read interminable Dickens novels, to which he was loyally devoted, and when Dylan was loyally devoted, no sentimental verbosities would change him, though he did bog down somewhere in *Little Dorrit*. He categorically refused to look at Proust, Jane Austen, Tolstoy, Dostoevski, and a lot of the obvious classics,

55

though I furiously asked him, how could he know he wouldn't like them, without bothering to look; but there is no doubt he knew all right. He probably knew, more than anybody, what he liked, and what he didn't like, and what he wanted, and what he didn't want; without, like most people, having to find out. Once again that fiendish element of his days being numbered, comes into it; and all that sickly, stinking stuff about: It had to be, there was no other way; the illogical, poets must die young, ruthless reasoning that made him follow, nobly and foolishly, that exorable pattern. And it was not necessary at all, not without that baby-snatching seduction: there was no hope, after that; to America.

In case my opinions reek of fanaticism, I should like to make clear two things: one, that had I been in Dylan's place, I should have reacted far worse, had my head, not only turned, but swivelling in a thousand fascinating rotating directions, my roots waving riotously overhead; whereas Dylan was, even at his worst, Dylan; and there was one part of him that nobody could get at, that was impregnable, untouchable, not of his own making, but handed down from generations of close-tied, puritanical, family tradition. Handed down from his father, that most unhappy of all men I have ever met; who did all the spade work of casting off the humble beginnings, bettering himself, assiduously cultivating the arts; and finished up a miserable finicky failure: while passing on to Dylan, on a heaped up plate, the fruits of all his years of unrewarding labour. To an outsider his step up the social ladder might not seem so impressive: the transition from farmhouse and railwaymen standards, to schoolmaster in a semi-detached suburban matchbox. But it made the leaping change from lavish rough comforts to pinched penny-pricing gentility; to the taxing position of being looked up to by the neighbours, therefore having to keep up the most trussed-in, belted, camouflaged and gloved system of appearances; instead of being so low you had not got to bother, and could wear and say what you liked, make as much noise, and enjoy yourself, without being stigmatized. No blue-blooded gentleman was a quarter as gentlemanly as Dylan's father. And, though Dylan imagined himself to be completely emancipated from his family background, there was a very strong puritanical streak in him, that his friends never suspected; but of which I got the disapproving benefit.

Those who only saw his bar-leaning, on, and on, and on story, with no detectable end, telling; would never credit that other punctilious, pettifogging niggler for detail, making such a fuss over the correct dress for me to wear for the Carmarthen market, I mean it, right down to gloves, stockings, shoes; and he would have preferred a hat, but knew that was too much, even for him, to ask of me. His ideal dress for a woman: black from head to foot, relieved with a touch of white, as a concession, a neat starched collar and impeccable cuffs: and the shoes not *too* high, nor *too* low: flaps, sandals, or boots, the most offensive; inconspicuous the key word, and tidily laced, with a prim bow. The final production the direct opposite of me: a politician's perfect secretary. And dandleable.

The other thing, in case there is any misapprehension of my attitude: the American people. To us, of the frozen north, as I always think of our chilblained island, it is very hard at first not to suspect such a basketful of warmth, generosity, and hospitality; but whether it springs pristine from the heart, or is a cultivated college art, it is equally pleasant; and should be taken at face value: appreciated, and responded to; not carped at, as some nasty people do. I am a great believer in whatever you say and do often enough, becoming true;

on a lesser scale, but the same line of thought, as the Catholic religion. And the individuals, when you learn to distinguish them: but that is nonsense on my part, they are easily distinguishable; have all the initial, too-good-to-be-trueness, and, as though that weren't enough, they add intelligence: and I don't mean just bright wiffs, but an all round, thorough, comprehensive education; and have not only read, but made theses on, all the books we should have, but never quite did, read. And this remarkable combination they cap with a boyish open enthusiasm; and, what surely is the height of friendliness and tact, which the crustiest crank is not proof against, the genuine desire, or as near as it is possible to get to it, to hear *your* opinion; and a simply stupendous hearing —dripping with sympathy, listening ability. And very soon, in spite of your stubbornest self, you will imperceptibly start softening down into a cushiony pulp, airtight and hermetically corked, under the neutralizing influence.

This is known as the American breaking-in process, which has slaughtered the health and spirit of many a gallant adventurer. But where, I asked myself, is the fly, the itch, the scabies of contention that makes these people fly in all directions, on frivolous errands, and never be still: that makes them put such untiring energy, though not, I think, deep pleasure in the Latin sense, into their amusements, and their zealous touching quest for culture? Perhaps it is just that ant of dissatisfaction that crawls insidiously under the skin, that drives them on to such lengths of munificence, magnificence, grandiloquence. That glosses over poverty, gives the lie to suffering; and makes even of death a grandguignol travesty.

For Dylan, more than anybody, this was a poisonous atmosphere: he needed opposition, gentle, but firm, constant curbing, and a steady dull, homely bed of straw to breed his fantasies in. Nobody ever needed encouragement less, and he was drowned in it. He gave to those wide-open-beaked readings the concentrated artillery of his flesh and blood, and, above all, his breath. I used to come in late and hear, through the mikes, the breath-straining panting: making much too much wind for an actor, which he liked to fancy he was, but admitted he hammed unrestrainedly; booming blue thunder into the teenagers' delighted bras and briefs. And I thought, Jesus, why doesn't he pipe down; they would be just as pleased with a bacon-rind of that rich tinker's spoils, sizzling over the flames.

Then the clustering round for autographs; the students' apple-polished, shining faces, with creaseless wonder: I should have been grateful for a pucker of consternation on those too smooth brows.

But this negligible element was swept aside by the sea of the matriarchs, surging glorious-plumed, perfumed, jewelled; chanting, exclaiming, declaiming; indomitably avalanching to drain the reflex twitches, faint spasms, from the exhausted corpse.

To the best, most patient, understanding wife, my position was not an easy one; but to me, stiff with rancour, my own teeming passions fermenting angrily inside me, it was a hanging execution of my all-important pride. I deliberately antagonized, said, almost inaudibly, the thing that hurt in the place that hurt; as though I was a rip-roaring delinquent, starved of love and light. When, as far as I can remember, what we suffered from most, was too much freedom, running wild; and the consequent inability to discipline ourselves or join, with any aptitude, a regulated social group. Whether I was loved or not never occurred to me: children do not know that they need love, and only later feel the lack of it. And

I am one of the renegades who think grown-ups need it more: that the older they get, and the less love they get, the more they need it: the more they are willing to sell their nothing for it.

I did not for a second resent Dylan's success, except that it took him away from me; I wanted him to have everything that was good for him, made him happy. But an essential condition of his happiness must be me: I had to be the thing that made him happiest. So when he started taking notice of other women: they had never bothered him before seriously; I cannot pretend I was serenely sweet-tongued. In America, they hunted singly, in pairs, and more often in packs, and as soon as one pack was downed and wiped out, from those limitless wide open spaces came fresh hordes, massing numberless, in the tracks of the old. They had never heard of that out-of-date claptrap that a woman should at least make a dissimulation of waiting for the man to make the first move. Not them, they were candidly, if not prepossessingly, spreadeagled, from the first tomtomed rumour of a famous name. They conducted their courting with the ferocity and tenacity of caged amazons; and nothing less than the evaporation of their prey would make them let go.

These thieves of my love, which I was so presumptuously sure was mine only, I bitterly, jealously resented, with all the primitive catfish instincts that I didn't even know were there, and the vile, sinking, retching lurch, that jealousy engenders.

Dylan felt as badly as me, in this respect, at the inconceivability to him of me even distantly contemplating anybody else; and he reacted more abominably than me; no cruelty or physical mutilation was too much, for such an unpardonable crime. It seems extraordinary to me now that we did not kill each other outright, we certainly got dangerously near to it, on those bloodthirsty vengeances.

I wish to God somebody would analyse out of me all the theories, kinks, and bed sores I am guilty of; it would be unadulterated heaven and peace to be without them, but not me. But who, may I ask, in their right senses, would want to stay me, not me, I am sure of that. And what do I know of heaven and peace? I only know they are the opposite of everything I am, and therefore must be good; that there should be nothing I am not prepared to see, hear and feel; that there are *no* certain things that are better kept out of sight; from a skinned rabbit to a Belsen camp. The drooling, spoon-fed imbeciles; the truncated, kindly, refinedly preserved, to save their feelings; it would not be ours, would it? from embarrassing attention: the half men, with brains awhirl, and no hands, the war heroes. And the caged, the barred, from animals to man made animal. However much I rail against my wrongs, I have that much sense left to know that my prison does not compare with the official prison: no sun, no water, no air. And, have I got to say this too, Dylan basely humiliated with the disgusting things he dreaded most; not one organ in his body working in its own right, without mechanical assistance: intravenal feeding, tubes attached blatantly to each vulnerable shy orifice; the head encased in a transparent tent, pumping oxygen into him; the eyes turned up, bulging, unseeing; the breath roaring like a winded horse pounding up a slope; and no Dylan there, no contact. Only the limp hands lying, separate, speaking to me. And everybody knowing it was hopeless and all over; that this was a farcical artificial prolongation of what had already gone.

But I am supposed to be in the island, writing my chatty book, with vivid descriptions, bright comments,

61

and interesting personalities; not in St Vincent's Hospital, Greenwich Village.

So now we must be dragged, though not much dragging was needed with Dylan and me, to the inevitable party, after the reading. I do not know what I expected, or wanted, from a party, but ever since I was a child I thought, and still cannot rid myself of the idea, that the gates of some exotic scintillating world would open, diametrically disconnected with my own. So when they turned out to be more stolidly plebeian, humdrumly golden-hearted, in spite of the gallons of frozen fire water that were being consistently poured down, than any stability, security, continuity I had ever known, I had a sense of astonished anti-climax. I was always waiting for something stupendous to happen, to change the whole course of my life; at the back of my mind this stupendous happening was me rising to my feet and electrifying the company with a masterpiece of inspired dance, the like of which had never been seen before. But before I could get myself into the state of not caring what I did, of being bold enough to let myself go, without stint or concern for the ill-fitting dignity of my wifely position, or the repercussing hereafter; I had to wolf down so many fast drinks, that by the time I was ready to take the floor, I could only turn in blind circles, with my skirt over my head. Not very edifying.

When Dylan was the lion, he sat, as though to the manner born, and, as though he had never sat otherwise; couched immovably in the guest-of-honour chair, with his disciples, mostly female, squatting at his feet, agogedly eager: anyone who has seen a spaniel waiting the call of the gun will know what I mean; to devour his next words; which came stumbling, haltingly, one on top of the other, in a broken, stuttering rush. While I, pinioned as far away as possible, was being politely sought out by kind, pitying, neither one thing nor the other, friends; and asked all about my children, their ages, and sexes, etc.; to which I answered in surly monosyllables. I wanted so much to be gracious; and could put on a first class Queen Mother act, on demand; that was the silly contradiction of it; but not with Dylan, not with him monopolizing every ear in the room.

He had the same dislike of me receiving any attention or limelight, not that this happened so frequently. Was this due entirely to a husband and wife relationship, or were we worse than most? It is a sobering thought, and not an inducement to lifelong shackles of tyrant habits and accumulating, threadbare-curtained detestation, when under the pressure of too long quilted intimacies, the dears and darlings become *dears* and *darlings*: 'Would you mind moving up, my *dear*, and giving me a little room in the bed.' This never happened to us, but we were nipped early.

But every now and then, through the indistingishable waves of gush, came a clear cut human being, as dear and familiar as a moth-eaten aunt, who had lain too long at the bottom of a trunk in the attic. No words were needed, the 'understanding' was immediate and mutual; we instinctively held together: a tiny oddly-assorted oasis, in a city of planes, and blocks and sinister sky-scrapers, harbouring millions of hiding lives; each with its separate fascinating drama to be unravelled. And these misfit friends of mine, yes, really mine as well, were not stereotyped, or made to measure: they were the artists, the pariah dogs, and, though I hate to have to say it, the much maligned bohemians. But the bohemians in America are not, by a very long well-creased leg, the same as that original romantic Parisian article, starving in a garret, in an atmosphere, reeking in equal proportions of beards, misunderstood genius, and plain filth.

Dylan and I fell between the two extremes; and though we both had a great loathing for poverty and squalor and did all we could, which was mostly talk, to get out of it, and achieve that ideal state of bourgeois respectability and armchair comfort we both craved; or to be exact, Dylan did; to me there was nothing between the barn and the Salon; we never quite, though we got pretty near, achieved it. It was the same with money: we spent hours planning all the sensible, civilized things we would do with it; eking it out on *moderate* enjoyment, like proper people; vowing and swearing before our Holy Maker, never again to indulge in those racketing wastes that wrought such havoc in us; and in which a good half of our lives was spent. But the valuable quality of moderation was totally lacking in both of us; in one was bad enough, but in both it was fatal. So when the eventual lump came: as far back as I can remember, we were living in hopes of a usually mythical lump coming to solve all our troubles, past and future; the feel of a couple of crinklers was so foreign, and so intoxicating to us, that an immediate celebration, and a riot of spending on all the things we had wanted so long, and a lot more we had not, but just could not resist; was one of those things that the best people simply *had* to do, and it never seriously occurred to us not to, in spite of the messes we got ourselves into. So the back debts went on pressing, only harder, getting steadily more voracious; and the future was laden with threats and wangling tortures: all the belittling intricacies of money worries. Poor nervous Dylan, who had inherited, besides his father's hypochondria, his acid pessimism for always anticipating the worst, suffered sleepless nights more than me. I had developed, through never having any, and my mother's lofty teaching, that it is vulgar to speak of money, a happy detachment from it, and, though nobody enjoyed the spending of it more, it was a solemn duty with me, yet I could never make myself feel it really mattered, or appreciate the value of it. And of course it was Dylan had the job of making it.

However, no more about dirty money: it is only important when you have none; and though it may not be everything, it goes a very long way towards blocking up the winter draught of age.

The American bohemians, as I was saying, though appearing to us as cellophane-wrapped, chic, slick, showroom models, had their flaws, failings, and irregularities. It was possible, on close observation, to detect a rent in the clothing, here and there, a rare darn, an occasional untidy bathroom, with strewn soiled linen, but never no bathroom at all. And, although there was a lot of talk about the cost of living, which was undoubtedly very high, and the necessity for crippling economies, nevertheless their apartments looked spacious and sumptuous to us, with beautiful central heating, that best of all inventions. There was always a stock of good whisky, and usually Californian wine, for frequent early cocktail times, and delicious appetizing delicacies to go with them. It was only in the richer houses that we suffered the indignity of iced water with our meals.

LL—E

VII

THERE is an intangibility about the houses of the rich;
I mean the deep, seriously embedded, religiously wedded
to money—the indecently moneyed few. They have
turned full circle, and are at great pains to disguise their
wealth, their heavy burden; which everybody is only too
willing to share the weight of; but nothing on earth would
make them part with an ounce of it. They sport a rustic
simplicity, string the beans, rough-cast the walls,
sprinkle sawdust on the floor; all at vast cost, labour,
and inconvenience to everybody; to get, as near as
money can bring them, to Christ's stable; provided that
the champagne is under the straw. And if they hang a
discreet painting, it is one of the freak, out-of-line works
of one of the accepted painters: designedly chosen by
one of the taste boys, with substantial profit to himself;
in order to mystify and intrigue, with their subtle
connoisseurship. Or something so modernistic it is
indiscernible; at most one small black, or if very temperamental and unsuppressible, three large, scarlet, dots,
pierced by a few jagged shrieking lines going nowhere;
and the rest of the extra large canvas generously
smeared in a substance closely resembling a baby's
motion. Or the odd burst breast suspended disconsolately over the dismembered tree; with strings of liver
and lights, intestinal innards slung, with equal lack of
aim, over an adjoining brick wall meticulously accurate,
which, for some obscurely profound reason, is standing

66

all on its own, with no detectable function except to give diagonal shade to a pair of very lonely down-at-heel boots. And yards and yards of desert sand, without a ripple or a wrinkle, stretching, in mute convolutions, behind.

I wish I could have used paint instead of words: I have about the same amount of amateur skill in each; because whatever you say in paint can be interpreted as something else, but the horrible words speak for themselves; unless, of course, you are a modern verse writer. And with what sincere, solemn interest Dylan would receive the shoals of bated breath poems presented to him, by ardent followers, who, unless my eyesight deceived me, had often artlessly copied down one of Dylan's poems, verbatim, interpolating an extra bone, or worm, or heron, in surprising places, to give it that extra touch of authenticity. Dylan always tucked them conscientiously away, in a fabulous portfolio for future reference, and feeling genuinely self-righteous as at a duty well done, never looked at them again. There were some that dated back to the early days of our marriage, and were still in a virginal condition of unthumbed preservation. And in the meantime the throbbing sources of these springs of song waited with palpitating impatience, and daily waning hope, for the shattering, or master-making, verdict.

If I ever hammered away at one of my dirges of despair, which I had to be at the bottom of the blackest pit before I dared attempt, and eventually made myself, with terrible nervous qualms, ill concealed by a bland, as I thought, non-committal face: it is very annoying, but has got to be recognized, that nobody is indifferent to their own creations, or they wouldn't do them; and everybody is beastly sensitive somewhere, but I still insist some are more so than others; Dylan would be very sweet, pick on a few nice words to quote, ignore the turgid dross, and say in all innocence: 'Why don't you make it into a poem, Darling?' What did he think I'd been slaving nights for? Then I would say: 'What is a poem?' and he couldn't tell me. I only wanted the rules, like in a piece of music, to follow, but he said there weren't any, you made your own rules; and it either was or wasn't a poem. Dylan incidentally was not moved to preaching against: after voraciously eating their good dinner, like me: the museums of the privileged classes. He settled down, perfectly at home, like a baby in a new and exciting play-pen, to play with and dissect the latest tinkling, spidery mobiles, vibrating with metallic strings and silenced gongs. Or to refashion more absurdly the once fashionable surrealist gadgets: hands and chains intermingling erotically; and wheelbarrows with golden padlocks; the telephone with a human, soapy, glazed, rather the worse for wear, papiermâché ear; the mouthpiece an alarming assortment of cannibal's teeth. But the arty-tarts that really struck the fear of God into Dylan were the mouse fur shoes: unfairly eclipsing the potency of the shrunken Indian heads.

(For Dylan had an abhorrence of the creeping, crawling animal vermin, summed up in the panic word: *mice*. To reassure him, people would say, when he was screaming like a stuck pig: not at the sight, that would have caused an all-out faint; but at the scrabbling behind the wainscot, the voracious rattling of paper as though they were lions at least: 'but they are only such small, little wee things . . . they can't hurt you.' But it was their very smallness that horrified him so much; and this was an authentic horror.)

We had our special group of steadies, whom I depended on a lot more than Dylan, as he was always on the move, hectoring to the raw thirst of neighbouring colleges;

while I was dumped pretty well, a not very sugary package, on their doorsteps. And here and now, as I always seem to be carping about something, I want to do official homage to them; for the truly noble, selfless way they put up with me; more than put up with me; they not only showed me goodness and kindness, as I have never been shown it before; but I sincerely think they enjoyed my company; not as Dylan's wife, but as I enjoyed theirs. I can't leave out that dim intermission of time, which was neither life nor death; when Dylan was fighting for his life; or, to be more accurate, his life was being fought for: he was never that keen on life, and ready, from the start, to relinquish it; and I was fighting to the death, to achieve death. I rumbled, and quaked, and erupted on the surface; yet my Caitlin volcano, snarling deep down, would not break, was too savage to crack.

This is where my little valiant Rose, my special chosen friend, adopted me; left her job to look after me, sent away her husband, as I affected a revulsion against the proximity of all men: perhaps it was real, but when I look back over this period of outrages, committed by me, and against me, I wonder how much was real, and how much play acting. But then the play acting is sometimes more convincing, and who is to say it is not real. It is hopelessly confusing trying to think straight about this brutal blot in time, because weapons of retaliation against hurt have nothing to do with the thinking brain. So my Rose took me in, and we lived alone, together in a strange, phosphorescent, half world, of night and day. Rose, who can't possibly have felt anything like me, had the gift of the chameleon: she coloured herself from head to foot in my mood of daft, distracted, irresponsibility. We lay for hours, in two oceans of beds, in the morning, with the blinds down, and the lights full on,

69

rambling on about early childhood, distant girlhood, past ambitions, foolish yearnings, anything far back, everything, except Dylan. Waiting, both incapable of lifting a finger, for David, her wise husband, to come, from where he had been banished to, to make us coffee, put it on the floor beside us, and as quickly and silently disappear again. After more indeterminate hours, we would start slowly moving about, up and down the long room, in flapping, shiftless garments, and bare, padding feet: pottering, uselessly tidying up, vaguely pulling back the covers, then pulling them limply forward again, turning on the bath, and forgetting to turn it off, starting to wash, and giving up in the middle, turning on the gramophone, and sinking back on the bed. Somewhere around English tea-time, and American second cocktail time, we were dressed and ready to go out. Holding tightly to each other, and tottering on our high heels, we emerged into the dazzling blaring streets, like winter blind squirrels blinking into the light. We visited the saloon bars, tried to eat, could not swallow: for the first time, I, normally at such pains to stop myself eating, found that the food just stuck in my throat and would not go down; but the rye and the bourbon went down only too easily, exacerbated the frayed, unhemmed, edges of feeling, Rose and I had so studiously avoided.

Suddenly, on empty bellies, and no sense at all, we were deliriously gay: there is no gaiety as gay as the gaiety of grief. Dylan always said he did not know what it was; sense of fun, yes, but gaiety: what Welshman has ever heard of that? Now *I* do not know what it is any more. So we went off to the big stores, handled, hypnotized, shelves of shining frippery, glowing baubles, tossed into the air myriads of sky blue, shocking pink, lime yellow, and rainbow striped panties; petticoats cascading, bubbling, foaming with frills, and much too pretty

70

to put underneath; tried on, all crazed, extravaganzas we had no wish or intention of buying. For once, my lust for dressing up did not function, I did not covet from the depths of my greedy being, all the tantalizing finery my lascivious eyes fell upon: I stood as cold, and as scaly as a crocodile, in the midst of so much, obnoxious to me now, glittering vanity.

When we got back to our nostalgic home, we found it was full of people waiting for us since time immemorial, that we had entirely forgotten having invited, if we had invited them at all. There was Lougé, who made every other poet look like a butcher: such a neurotic bundle of cuddlesome sweetness, and charm of face and manner. I asked myself where was the bottom of this seductive honey-pot; the brine and gallstones that made the poems; but I need not have worried, they were safely tucked away in prosperous Bronxville, floating in mother cushioning, pet-pampering, family asphyxiation. And, though he made regular sorties to New York, on what, to him, were ghastly debauches; he never failed to catch the last train home to mother. And he talked earnestly, if a shade half-heartedly, about getting a job, and getting away from it all; but he was sitting far too prettily, in suburban curtained opulence, to snap that steel elastic cord. Nobody in the world was more generous; I felt happy as soon as I saw him.

There was Malcolm B., somebody whom it is quite impossible to talk about in a few words, but it is also quite impossible to leave him out. For us he was more a symbol of divine powers, than a pedestrian person, and held a place, uniquely distinct, from any of the people we met afterwards. If ever he reads this, which may all the saints preserve him from, I can hear the creaking, and rending of his tensed, humming-bird delicate eardrums. We both loved him; but I fear that the *we* and the *both*, will hurt him more in the quick than any calculated criticism I could fabricate against him. All right, I will cut them out and put instead that Dylan loved him in his special personal way; and I loved him, in my special impersonal way. Because at no point in our previous incarnation or the next, could we conceivably find one congenial blade of grass on which to meet, except through Dylan; and there is no more unsatisfactory relationship, than that which subsists on the presence of a third person, more especially when that third person is dead. However, my appreciation of Malcolm B. has nothing to do with all these unimportant emotional conflicts; to me he is a creature, certainly not from this world, and not formed of mortal clay, but from some prehistoric planet, undiscovered by men, and of a translucent liquor, solidified into moon opaque, cloud-gargoyled shape.

Did I say Lougé was a neurotic? By comparison he was a square rigged, ten-foot beamed, hundred-per-cent business man; though I have a sneaking suspicion they are the biggest neurotics of the lot, and guiltily hide secret poems in the recesses of their desks. But Malcolm B. was in an air-conditioned stratosphere of his own; he had outstripped the prevalent nervous disorders a long time ago, and lived in a purely artificially-stimulated vatican city of his own, which to us radiated serenity. He carried with him everywhere a suitcase of magic tablets, without which, he assured us, taken in ordered rotation, he would magically fall apart and disintegrate. No doubt, as he intimated, he seethed underneath, and his private life was fraught with excruciating, unprintable dramas; but externally he was smooth, affable, wonderfully polite, in warm caressing tones, sunken with understanding; and so visibly sensitive, that he made me feel like a rhinoceros rooting in an exquisite bed of flowers.

When he left us in New York on his frequent long drives
—by long I mean a distance that we might, after endless
planning and preparation, do once a year in England—
to different, widely spaced colleges, to do his teaching
job; we felt unfairly deserted, and pathetically lost
without his support. So much had he come to be not only
the guardian of our money, which, we grumbled, he
never gave us enough of: while *he* never ceased to be
horrified by our doubled spending capacity; but the
guardian of our rags and tatters of fast-diminishing
senses. Then, out of nowhere, he would suddenly be
there, at an identical, knocking-it-back, tripe-talking,
sex-flapping party; and at once we dropped the tom-
foolery and felt safe and good again.

There was his friend Rollie; the least American in
the vacuum-cleaner sucking-up sense, of anybody we
met; she was most refreshing after the douches of gush
that were later released over Dylan's unbowed head. I
wanted nothing better than to spend the rest of my life
in her cool, unpossessive company: but let me quickly
add, that this touching sentiment was not reciprocated
by her; for she was much too independent and self-
contained to betray, across her dead body, the leanest
shade of preferential feeling. Even in the Dylan crisis,
when everybody seemed to be going mad in their various
ways, or was it only me magnifying them, I never saw her
ruffled once; and it slightly annoyed me that nothing
could make her show one sign of weakness. But I was
not fool enough to think she felt nothing: she simply
believed in not showing her feelings; and was one of
those rare people who did, and how few there are, what
she believed in. I shall never forget, after that futile
church service: a mealy-mouthed compromise between
literary preciosity and the overriding fear of making
fools of themselves by too much musical pomp and

ritual: when Dylan would have obviously preferred the typical blood and thunder Welsh hymns passionately shouted over him; as though it mattered what he would have preferred; seeing, through that blue of melting faces and outstretched hands, Rollie, standing upright and clean cut, courageous as a Viking, on the outside of the crowd; and I stumbled towards her.

And I cannot forget either the Welsh Society coming to visit me, still wandering about in my sackcloth at Rose's; and how, even in that state of abysmal disadvantage, I could not help being impressed by the endearing cardboard formality of their pinstripe suits, their industriously polished shoes, their squeezed to extinction collars. After several generations in America they had not lost one intonation of the guiding Welsh principles, nor contaminated with a drawling slur their chanting up-and-down accents. So, as a matter of sacred duty, they had to be present, in a body, at the death, if not in the life, of their greatest bard. After a tremendous amount of palavering, and skirmishing round the fragile, handle-with-care, subject, they solemnly presented me with a small cheque, collected from the extensive Welsh community.

There was Oscar, the outrageous, whom we shocked our better friends by being so fond of. They were not able to understand that it was possible, not to be blind to his shortcomings, but to like him, not in spite of them, but rather because of them. It is one of those unfair manifestations that the imperfect are invariably the more amusing people; there is nothing very amusing, unhappily, about being perfect. And whether all the derogatory stories about him are true or not, the fact remains that he did more for us, in the practical ways that really matter: that is to say, going through fantastic machinations, involved conferences, sparing no trouble, or dirty work, for himself, to obtain for us frequent sums of money; which also continued, even more invaluably, in our lean days in Wales, constantly saving our skins in the nick of time. When Dylan was away on his travels, he was very kind to me, taking me to the popular movies, and patiently sitting in dives with me: showing me the working man's New York. I will not believe he did it all, just because I was the poet-of-the-moment's wife. When hostesses, the host never seemed to count, complained bitterly, in spite of elaborate precautions, that it was impossible to have a party without Oscar; far from finding this positively noble nerve offensive, I could not but admire him, for finding so dismal a cause worth such a big expenditure of Oscar guts and pride. And, speaking for myself, my first anxiety when arriving at a party was: 'Where is Oscar?' and if, though this only happened very infrequently, he was not there, the party was over for me. He was our Petrouchka, our devil's mascot.

There was Ruthven, a good example of the nervous, jumping, guttercombing Scotsman made good. What a change from the early London days when we used to know him: gabbling, penny-counting, the shy man's too hysterical cackling laugh. But, now I come to think of it seriously, hardly changed at all, only gained in assurance. Proving, and what a pleasure to be able to say so, that it is possible for encouragement and good living to be positively beneficial. He had expanded, not only physically, but mentally, giving to others a pleasant warming confidence, rather than seeming in need of it himself. He married a beautiful wife, not destitute by any means: a happy combination which, to the naïve observer in the States, grows two a penny on trees.

Another of the dropped lucky, who got out the right side of the bed, was Mr Lye; full of Australian vigour, and ideas which had never quite materialized; he also acquired such another paragon. She was not only good-looking, with a tidy slice of her own, but gave him a luxurious studio in which to practise his film innovations. So he spent all the day, happy as a mechanic flat on his back under a car, experimenting, and tinkering, and juxtaposing, with lights, and effects, and drunken bubbles deliriously bursting all over the screen. While she went cleverly marketing, cooked delicious meals, and I am not at all sure she did not have a job as well, to help the budget. This set-up is not at all unusual; though a great emancipator myself out of America, I found it more than I could comfortably swallow in action. The picture of the husband, in a jovially flowered pinny at the sink, or petulantly flicking a feather duster, or placidly, and probably much more competently, changing the baby's nappies; has no visual appeal for me; I revert illogically to the bad old-fashioned days and prate of unseemliness. Saucepan boys they are called in Wales, and, though I am all for the men sharing the menial jobs, it is impossible not to despise them when they do.

Dylan was never guilty of this particular; yes, it cumulatively amounts to one; vice. The most he ever attempted was a super fry-up of all the leftovers: spattering, in the process, the walls, the floor, and even the ceiling with flying scalding fat; producing in the end, as he invariably forgot it to go on with his book, a black, charred pulp which he smothered in 'Daddie's' sauce, and swilled down with fizzy cyder for breakfast. As for minding babies while I went out, that was unthinkable and against his strongest codes: which he never once made an exception to. Any small repair or adjustment that needed a handy man, was equally out of the question; he was as useless as a penguin with his hands, except for the one purpose. Nobody was ever more of a

one-purpose, undeviating person, from the very beginning; knowing exactly what he wanted, and what he
could do. No high flown aspirations or hesitating doubts;
but a dangerous lack of sticking-to-it power. As I was
nearly as bad, and impractical as well, it is no wonder
nothing ever functioned with us in our homes, and we
got ourselves into such disastrous messes.

Rose and I, frivolously gurgling, in our bath of apathy,
would remark: 'Why doesn't Ann Lye come, to tell us
what to do?' No sooner said, than the door would open,
and in she would come: already up for five hours, done all
the marketing, and preparations for the day's entertainment; besides a couple of hours' typing. These energetic
super-women always have typing to do; it is a most
important convention, which remains one of the blessedly
unplumbed mysteries. But, devil take it, those un-
drugged, clean, matitudinal hours have got to be killed
somehow. She would immediately fabricate for us, in less
than five minutes, a sustaining snack; hustle us out of
bed, create order in our chaos, while appearing, at the
same time, calmly static. We gazed in adoration at this
celestial vision reflecting our imperfections, and wished
she would stay with us perpetually. But she disappeared
as suddenly as she had come; and left us, abandoning all
pretence now of getting up, to talk about the wonder of
her far into the night. I still have the jeans and the pearls
she gave me, symbols of her character: tough as a jean,
and rare as a pearl; and out of all the glamorous trash I
brought back with me, the jeans were the only suitable
wear for my mud-dump; and the pearls were the finishing refinement for my cruel black outfit, which I knew
would please the Welsh, if nobody else.

VIII

So my party was drawing to a close; I do not mean just this party but the one I had from the moment I arrived to the moment I left; which, in a sense, was one long, riotous, suicidal revel. I threw myself into it with every ounce of strength I had, hoping subconsciously I suppose, through the sheer weakness of excessive excess, to escape the consequences lying viciously in store for me. I might have spared myself the trouble for all the good it did me, and knowing my unkillable self as I do; no interlude of drowsy, memory lapsing, forgetfulness for me: I had it coming to me, and it came; bang wallop, like all hell's hammer-tongued flames it did.

My experience of Bins is not extensive, but more than sufficient. How far can I go down the musty corridors of insanity without getting to the end? madly far enough. The primary, most noticeable symptom, perhaps, is the irresponsible hilarity that prevails; not to be confused with happiness. It is because they have ceased to differentiate between good and evil: it is the relief of having the burden of choice removed. There is somebody else to perform that irksome job now; and, Jesus, are they going to play them up! The suicidals are gay as skipping crickets; the paranoiacs sport and giggle in the womb; and the pricked schizophrenes crack apart like scalded chestnuts.

True, there are those near-naked effigies, glued to windows, perched on radiators, with the shrouded immutability of prehistoric birds, looming silently from sunk ages. But I dare not tread, with my prodigious ignorance, in that forbidden territory. And I will ignore the droolers and bed-despoilers, hoping they have gone beyond the limitations of shame.

So there was I, seeing and hearing cut-glass acutely; the undeniably sane freak among the chattering starlings. My madness: an untutored broken heart. My punishment: a straitjacket. This house of salutary correction in America, to repose the frayed nerves. Just re*lax*, dear: in your iron cot behind bars; and have a nice *long* sleep.

I am not saying they are worse there; there is a type of mass brutality, accompanied by raucous joviality on the part of the brawny female keepers, jangling their giant predatory keys with sadistic glee, which may be less mentally cruel than the genteel pretence of the considerate English: that there is no such thing as a crude derangement of the senses; merely a temporary change of address for the sake of the sea-view. But the worst element to me of both systems is being studiously ignored, not being treated at all, for anything. Any amount of electric shocks would be preferable to that humiliating ignominy. I began to feel terribly out of it, shunned for being sane, and yearned to be a rip-raving 'case'. But, if I was not worth treating, why was I there at all? They kept rubbing it into me with a gloating satisfaction, how lucky I was not to have been sent to the vast State Asylum, where nobody paid, and nobody, once caught, came out; and the conditions had to be seen to be believed. I was not as grateful as I should have been, and went so far as to grudge the high payment of my enforced 'posh' establishment. I wondered who was so altruistic, or so desirous of having me out of the way, as to be responsible for it.

But since all things end in the end, though they may

79

take an unchartable time doing so; it might have been days or years for all I knew; I only knew my lifetime had ended and suffering had begun in earnest. The disgusted authorities told me crossly I did not respond, though they had done their best to make me *comfortable*; so I was removed. But is there anyone, so perverse seriously, they respond favourably to bolts and bars and bullying; lost on a barren moor of no love?

It is conceivable that this futile stunt did less than nothing to help the restoring process, though I admit I was not guiltless in provoking the protection of the law. I was possessed of ten thousand ravaging demons, whose passionate intention was to hurl themselves, full tilt down the steepest precipice. But although I visualized this dive in so many annihilating guises, and it seemed merely an extension of my cascading mind; yet, when I was poised on the vacillating verge, in went my heels, and a nagging know-all's voice from inside started to mock me: 'nothing will kill *you*; they'll have to shoot you.' So after these abortive trials, I felt cursedly immune from all dangers. No, it was no use pretending; no swift satisfying end for me; I should savour laboriously the stench smouldering from the capitulating years.

I tried to put out of my mind the knowledge of the boat, and Dylan's box in the hold; I even managed craftily to postpone the sailing date. But these unwanted chastisements have a habit of catching up on me, as though, it felt, I had been specially singled out for dedicated punishment; and the day came, as days infuriatingly do. I had trouble before getting out of the bed in the morning; but on this day, I did not have trouble: it was simpler than that, I simply could not move, to save the soiled tail of my life. The room next door was full of kind sympathetic people, with presents from their sore hearts, come to see me off; still I could not move.

Did I talk about my neurotic friends? Well, is there anything more neurotic than the body muscularly refusing to function, because the will does not want to? But at last I was hauled from the bed, by a conflagration of women, headed by Ann Lye; put on my feet, bathed, dressed; and, still inanimate, sodden, limp from indistinguishable hangovers, faced the tottering up and down before my eyes company. They too saw something of what I felt, looked down abashed, dropped pretences of jollity, and we shambled, it seemed aimlessly, off. Darling Lougé was still bravely carrying the champagne in a bucket of ice, and I was clutching on to David, Rose's husband, as the most stable flesh and blood there. He had that animal naturalness that belongs by rights, but not often in twisted strung-up life, to simple people; or is acquired deliberately by sophisticates: he was somewhere between the two, but more simple, I trusted, than sophisticated.

We piled into the tiny cabin, hysterically gabbling the last minute panic protestations; my brain was a numb, shuddering, nine-tenths drowned, mongrel whimpering dog; that squirmed and wagged its tail, when patted, with no volition of its own. There was that impeccable Biddy, another of our special friends; as pert, prim, and spring fresh, as a rain-washed meadow of daisies. It was hard to associate bookish intelligence with that dewy bud of a head, but she was exceptionally so; wrote herself, and taught, English you may be sure, and most surprisingly, was funny as well. With very little money of her own, she was a great one for giving presents; and bought me a lovely china Mexican pig money box, and basket, that I had long coveted. But charm and generosity are two of the gifts that Americans have a prerogative of.

And poor Herb, one of the serious drinkers; I only

call him poor in the affectionate sense, but, now I come to think of it, anybody who drinks seriously is poor: so poor, poor, extra poor, me. He was on his knees, his arms round my legs, as though clinging, for dear life, to the ultimate straw of departing Dylan. They had done a lot of boozing together; Dylan liked him for his apparent lack of intellectual pretensions; don't tell me he was an eminent critic all the time? And with him Dylan did not have to play the poet: they were no more than anonymous buddies. There is a brotherliness about a drinking person, which is coldly lacking in the straight and narrow enemies of drink; the difference between the two is more marked than nationality or belief: it is an opposite species altogether. It is against the unwritten laws of congeniality for them to mix. For me, a man who does not drink is distinctly indecent; as Maupassant said of a man without a moustache (though I emphatically do not agree with him about that): like an egg without salt. And the mere thought of going near a man who is not mellowly pickled, and whose breath reeks of his native fleshy self, is squeamishly unpalatable to me.

And Rose, her compact, hour-glass waisted, pint-pot filling figure, wedged tight up against the cabin wall; seemed to be getting smaller and smaller, and further and further away from me . . . like Alice after taking the shrinking medicine. I wanted to call her back, to howl to her to stop, to come with me; but nothing came out, I stared tongue-tied as at a statue.

Then the hooter went for the visitors to go ashore; and there was a relieved rush and pandemonium to escape. I was left mad; drunk; heartbroken; and, for the first time, horribly alone; in the middle of the morning; in the middle of the sea; and in the middle of Dylan and me: me and my box, down below, that I was bringing home.

Did I say alone, that was an optimistic mistake; at

least alone I could rip and tear at my raw entrails, press and bury my sight in their steaming hot hurt. I was lying huddled in not wanting: not wanting to be me, not wanting to do what I had to do, to go where I had to go, wanting *no* part in this tragic drama, which, for no good reason, had hooked on to me; when in walked a woman. Not a nice ordinary comfortable woman, of a homely age, but the kind that terrifies me most: young, suavely polished, metallically smart, always possessing just the right casual garment to change into. She sat, in an elegant négligé at the dressing table, nonchalantly manicuring her nails; dabbing delicately her lilywhite temples, and behind her shell-pink ears, with an exclusive scent of exquisite bouquet. Serenely impervious to the black crumpled figure, tear-stained and glowering at her, she emitted a faint moan of exasperation. No, she was not conducive to inspiring confidence; and, in my dismal abandonment, she doubly highlighted my discrepancies of dress; bulging monster bags of unrecognizably stuck together refuse of my visit; and my savage barbarity of behaviour. So this was the partner that had been relegated to me for the rest of the journey: as she herself may well and more justifiably have said about me; after stipulating so earnestly to the dear little, sweet little, British Consulate in New York, that I *must* be alone to muster my fleeing senses together. They were so super-tactful, diplomatic, well-bredly sympathetic; and all the staunch, loyal, enduring British qualities rolled into one; that I had implicit faith in them. They murmured soft nothings, indeed; in hushed tones: how *well* they understood, of *course* it should be done, for me not to worry about anything, they would see to *everything*. They did; then quietly, without giving me any warning, played this truly bastard trick on me.

I cursed them with the studded nails from the bottom

83

of my boots; but what good was that to me at sea? Then something went stiff with refusal in me at the prospect of five days' confronting that creamily elegant woman. I left the cabin, and never went back in. To achieve my precious privacy I had to deliberately stage a public breakdown and fits; but I was getting accustomed to the rôle now, and it came almost spontaneously. It is merely a question of choice of deaths. So, glossing over that not very delectable episode, I was locked in the hospital, somewhere in the bows, in the bowels of the ship, and not let out for three whole tossing days.

But I had got what I sought, which, at this point in my up-and-down career, was more important than anything else to me; so I ought not to grumble, which has never stopped me yet. On the first day that I was let out, wandering aimlessly into the hold, I came on a bunch of sailors, eating their lunch off a large box; with beer bottles and coats, and cards strewn all over it. Without being told, I knew at once that it was Dylan; and that, if it was possible for him to enjoy, he would have enjoyed that. But, in spite of dear sweet reason, it made me feel queer, when I was being stuffed on gigantic U.S.A. steaks that stuck in my throat, in the sumptuous dining saloon; and I tried to understand why I should be here, and him there. What had he done? or more pertinently, what had I done; not done; or undone?

I shall cut out the stilted drabberies of the return to England, where nobody ever says what they mean: and by denying feeling, kill it off stone-cold at the roots; but go on and on talking about the abominable weather instead. It is a lot easier, I get very worked up about it myself; and perhaps it is all that matters eventually. It was impossible to believe, now that I was pancaked back home, that all those glaring, garish, things had so lately happened to me. From the mortuary I never got

84

to, but said I *must*: it was one of the exceptional occasions when my nerve failed me; to the presentable deathhouse; where the corpses are dressed up, made up, and pumped up, with some kind of chemical to colour and preserve them. There I did get; but he was not there either; less there than anywhere: I looked and looked, and touched, but it was no good; he would not come to me. There was no telling it was him had been there; were it not for my exhibit of irrefutable evidence, that followed me wherever I went. Whenever I was being extra bad, I said to myself: if it had been the other way round, Dylan would have been twice as bad. But of course it could not have been the other way round; it was one of those ugly preordained things that *had* to happen this way round. More than that I do not know; but there is no doubt Dylan would have made a better job than me of killing himself: for damnation he has done it has he not?

Now, dropping this obsessive subject, with unanimous relief, I shall take a flying leap back to the island, where I should have been all the time; and where, at this instant, I am sitting wrapped in all my coats and socks, in my new house with a stone floor, built for heat; and perishing with the cold; while an icy island wind blasts all round it. Only two days ago I was bathing in the calm clear sea, with the cat's paw waves gently kneading the shore, and lying in the winter sun, which is about perfect heat for us frozen-up northerners; so the biting contrast is appalling.

IX

THE place, and position, are an Italian dream: high up above a beautiful bay, where I bathe, and have entirely to myself; not counting the sneakers and peepers, who squat in the bushes above to get an eyeful of stray breast or bum. But I have decided to ignore them, and allow these illicit glimpses, as long as they keep far enough away, or all my pleasure would be gone. After all, it is not so much to give and harms nobody. I only start shouting when one gets too near; but it makes me self-conscious all the same, and spoils my laborious peace. I think, when afterwards sitting on my terrace, trellised with vines, and looking down through the superbly leaden, or is it more gunmetal, olive trees; definitely my favourite trees; more terraces of vines; past the solitary overhanging pine tree, that makes a child-drawn circle of shade in the middle of my bay; and into the wide open, blue-eyed, staring back at me sea: anybody but me would be content with this. The bottle of red wine in front of me, and the long bread, the hard parmesan cheese; the mortadella, pomodori, and finocchi. There have been moments, when all the elements combined to create pure contentment; but how rare; there was nothing wrong with the elements very often, but the unyielding acid in me.

One day, for no special reason that I can remember, I suddenly felt whole again; and God, what a change. I was a new person, somebody I had forgotten a long time ago; I wanted to sing, and jump, and hug everybody, and kiss them. But it only lasted a day, then the wind came again and sent me shivering back where I had come from.

All this time Colm had been going to his asylum (*asilo*, as they not very encouragingly call the infant convent school), and I had taken one further perilous step, by leaving him there to lunch, which meant just soup; except that Italian soup is not quite the same as Windsor Brown; with extras supplemented by the mother. On the first day I went to great pains to get him the correct little cardboard case, tin plate, cup and spoon; and put in all the bits and pieces he liked best, including his special bananas; only to find, when I went to collect him later, he had been given the wrong case, full of cheeses and stuff he would not eat; and nearly broke his heart, watching the other boy eating his bananas. I nearly broke mine too; the baffling bewilderments of children, when they are transplanted from one familiar environment, to a frightening strange one, without knowing why; or worse still, the callous initiation into boarding school, which, to me, was the cruellest suffering; have the same quality of poignant unbearableness, as blinding cicadas to make them sing, clipping the wings of birds, tying cans to dogs' tails, leading cats on strings, tripping up cripples, tying goats' legs together, emptying nests of eggs, strewing the fledglings, caging any wild thing. And Colm, with his fair curls, novitiate's round white collar, and buttoned-tight-down-the-back black check tunic; with his stumpy trousered and booted legs coming out below, looked such a story-book angel of innocence, among the sloe-eyed, crafty by comparison, already mature natives. But this did not prevent me afterwards from half-killing him for some act of un-mitigated fiendery, far more imaginative than anything

87

the naïve darkies could have dreamed of perpetrating.

At nights we clung together, like the white haired, shipwrecked, ancient mariner and son; and this scrap of Dylan contact was both comforting and disturbing to me. With all Colm's demands and disturbances, I did thank thankless God, because there was nobody else to thank, he was there. He kept me on the move, tied me to certain times; and most of all, gave me a chance to meet the people, whom otherwise I would have had no excuse to talk to. Without him I am sure I would have walked straight over the nearest mountain, into an impenetrable mist, like Oates in the Antarctic, and never been seen again.

One of his near grown-up, but in the Italian sense of the word, completely grown-up friends, was Joseph; although he was only eighteen, three years older than my eldest son. He was a beautiful boy, and I liked him at once; a different type from the pretty boys who spent all their waking time, except for the sacred ritual of eating: (the leading question was always, 'Have you eaten yet?' if they had not, they could not take a drink, because it would hurt the stomach; and if they had, they said, with a pained *moue*, that they had already eaten); *passegiaring*: the only word for this full time Italian occupation, along with window-gazing, up and down the main street. Joseph did plenty of that too, when he had the chance, but in the week he had to work very hard: from six in the morning to four in the afternoon; in the iron mines, where most of the men worked, for very little money. This early necessity to earn his living, combined with the 'toughness' of the work, had given him an attractive grave hardness, sitting awkwardly on his extreme youthfulness, which, in spite of himself, would burst irrepressibly through on off-moments.

I asked him to look after Colm, while I went to my Italian lesson, with the Englishman's wife; which he did very well, and willingly. And, may I be struck down dead this instant, if this is a word of a lie; I never had an inkling of foreboding, that he might appear in the fantastic rôle of a lover. For one thing my vanity balked at such an absurdity, and I did not fancy myself as a haggard, rabid, avid randy dowager combing the Riviera for young blood. I had plenty of babies of my own, and had no inclination to snatch any more. My dignity was sorely troubled, but then, he was very, very sweet; and it seemed equally absurd to refuse to go about with Colm's friend. Fair play, it never occurred to me, that by making friends with Colm, these charming boys may have had, at the back of their calculating minds, the possible future savoury bite of me. And this manœuvring, if it were so, was not even flattering to me; since all the other seductible women were firmly locked up in their houses; and I was the only bit of procurable shoddy goods, on the market.

With Joseph I never felt that, and I am sure it was not true, though I am great at blind faith: he was so serious-minded and studious. His chief interest was to improve his English, and I could not make him talk Italian to me enough: it sounded with him, more mellifluous, more sonorous, more captivating, than anybody else's . . . which I might have guessed were certain ominous signs.

So we went walking together, the three of us; in the boat, where he looked wonderful, lazily rowing, with contained power, over the bouncing waves; to the beaches, where his comical terror at wetting his feet, damped momentarily the glowing picture of him; to the mountains, and the goats, and the herbs; and the beds of dry straw. And so, it involuntarily happened. Between the stalactite separateness of two people, and the first tentative gesture of intimacy, stretches a boundless plain of thorny distance, that appears insurmountable; but the instant that the two bloods meet, there is no stopping the heady, rushing upwards course together; and all the agonized constraints are swept away in the warm flooding; and laughed at, as ridiculous trifles, childish nonsense.

This state of affairs was far from pleasing to me; the last thing I wanted was a repetition of growing pains, from centuries ago, but still horribly clear. It brought back sensations I hoped never to suffer again: going weak at the knees, the stomach turning over, and dropping down, the heart thumping in the throat, a dizzy spinning of sickness, and an incurable impulse to bolt, at the sight of him. Was it fair he should subject me to this lowly pantomime, after the rigours I had undergone? Not even know he was doing it, that was my sole shred of comfort. All the time hammering into my head were those pathetically insufficient eighteen years, making a silly farce of the situation. Love can bear anything better than ridicule. But I could see the crude workings of nature behind it; she was sick to death of this persecuted, on-the-defensive, barbed world, I had entrenched myself into; and was making a strong counter-offensive against it: by offering me, so disarmingly, all the good happy things, I had thought lost to me for ever. But nature, being her jolly haphazard self, had attached a few insuperable snags, to her bountiful gifts; and I had got to the crook in my stony road, where I viewed with the gravest suspicion, anything pleasant that might inadvertently happen to me. I experienced an inexplicable guilt at taking something that did not belong to me: waiting, snail-shelled, for the gleeful foot to trample me; and it never failed in its ultimate trampling.

In this phenomenally childish affair, because, in this respect, I am ashamed to say, I am extremely childish too; which did harm to nobody, and good to both of us; there were fresh complications, disapprovals, and taboos from outside; making me feel as wicked a sinner as in Wales. Mostly from The Church, who was undoubtedly going mad. I had already been made to realize sorrowfully that my first estimation of him was lavishly 'too good to be true'; such idealistic saints, as I had painted him, do not run hotels, sit in a big office of the municipio all morning, and, more sinisterly, but equally in keeping, become Fascist heads in wartime. But with all his pompous pretensions to correct behaviour, viced respectability, and phantasy class; he still remained more like 'Juno's Paycock' than the stuffed-shirt turkeycock he aspired to be. And, mercifully, could not, with all his determination to rise above his clod-hopping plodding brothers, rub out, at all successfully, his inborn lovableness. But, since I was his accepted friend in front of the town, it became my duty, of necessity, to redound to his credit; which meant, in his language, that I should behave as he saw fit, according to his tightlaced rules. And since his rules allowed me to speak to no one but himself, his family, the Englishman and his; it left me, had I followed them implicitly, a genteelly thin social time.

When I complained about the lack of company to him, he collected a bunch of the more well-to-do female gentility, and brought them along to meet me. A more constrained meeting, with less to say to each other, and no means of saying it, with polite unwillingness on both sides; could scarcely have been cooked up more daintily. While he, the broad, tolerant, benefactor of mankind, sat beaming at the end of the table, not saying a word; but thoroughly convinced, that at last he had got me into my correct milieu; and all was well with the prosperous world. But it was not so well as all that: it was a bit late in the day to launch me into a society, that I had spent my life avoiding; so, though I politely acquiesced to his wishes, I also quietly went my own way; and I was not prepared, yet, to relinquish Joseph. The boy who said he would accept nothing, and was afraid of nothing: I seem to remember saying that myself, once.

One night, after supper, when Colm was in bed *and* sleeping, I went out, for the first time, walking alone with Joseph; not on the main road, but into the country. When I got back, after about an hour, I was met by warning shouts. Carabinieri, who have no resemblance to policemen, patrolling the streets, and The Church tearing up and down, on his motor bike, like King Lear riding his madness. So clutching my briary coat about me, I put on my best Queen Mary act, and head high, on stilts, attained the hotel: where my troubles were by no means over. The first thing I saw was Colm, wrapped in a blanket, being nursed by The Church's wife; and I knew, for a positive fact, that they had forcibly hauled him out of bed to dramatize my disgrace. Then when I got to our room, the man followed me in, and cursed and reviled me, as no sewer-swimming strumpet had ever been cursed and reviled before. In fluent Italian oaths, pointing with deranged persistence at my clothes: at tiny clinging burrs and brambles; and, though I did not know the meaning of the words they made themselves very disgracefully felt. There was one in particular that kept recurring: 'Vergogna, Vergogna!' which sounded the whoriest Babylonian slut; but which I discovered afterwards in the famous dictionary was comparatively harmless, no more than: 'shame, shame'. Perhaps the Italian shame is greater than ours.

However, the 'filthy' significance of 'Vergogna' was

92

made amply clear to me later on by the whole family: I was made to eat my shame, and grovel. If I went to the kitchen to ask for anything, I was met by downcast eyes; and The Church strutted, stuck his belly out, and would not talk to me at all, assuming an expression of exaggerated, sneering disgust; if I barely touched his sleeve, and said, 'Please . . .' he shook himself, as though bitten by an adder. The limit of his pained utterance, for over a week was: '*Signora, prego.*' To think I expected civilized relaxation; I began to hanker for Laugharne as an exotic Istanbul. However hard I tried to laugh this golden halter off, told myself it was not serious, that nothing could touch me now; yet so potent is the malignancy of public opinion; will I ever stop fighting it? that once again I felt like a fox on the run. What is more, The Church, with all his ties, pulls, strings, and telephone services, had me just where he wanted me: useless for me to say what right had he over me; at his protective mercy. Whatever I did, I was playing straight into his hands; so he openly and ruthlessly blackmailed me. Not only was he Paycock and Lear, but now had taken on the sinister guise of Count Fosca; he led me to the head of the Postal department and poured out, very fast, at the top of his voice, all his denunciations of me, and my lack of deportment, sparing no details. He used this unfortunate man, with a smattering of French; who was obviously utterly nonplussed, giving me despairing winks, passing on titbits of the discourse, and trying vainly to smooth him down; as interpreter. There was no reason why it should ever have ended had not the constant exasperated screams of Colm eventually intervened. My position was made no stronger by the crude fact that I was living on money borrowed from The Church; and I owed him for the hotel. Thus it had been all through my life with Dylan: never able to pay the necessary amount, at the necessary time; and I did hate the ignominy of it.

One afternoon, as I was on my own in the house, pretending to write: looking back at what had gone before, and asking myself, not only, is the writing utter trash? but, am I an utterly cheap person?—when along strolled Pietro. He was one of the professional glamour boys, deliciously pretty, famed as a Don Juan; making me feel like the proverbial lasting-for-ever leather of hide-bound England. And, though I was brimming with admiration for his seductive arts; making love at that hour in the afternoon, in the crotchety mood I was in, was too incongruous to contemplate. No two people, from opposite ends of the globe, can have been further apart. So, after arguing with him, and trying to persuade him to go, without being too nasty as he was so soft and tender, I left him in the house and went outside, making a show of working at the table there; and hoping this would make him give up, and tiptoe delicately away.

At this moment, there was an impatient rattling at the outer gate, which I had locked, to keep people out; and I hardly had time to whisper agitatedly to Pietro that people were coming, when in strode The Church, having got through the same hole in the hedge, with a look of furious suspicion on his face. He ordered me to unlock the gate at once as he had brought along the aforesaid quartet of Rio society to pay a social call, and have tea with me. In a dithering trance of fear, I obeyed and let them in, muttering vague mixed greetings. In the meantime, I could hear The Church going through the house: there were only three rooms; like an enraged bull, opening and slamming doors. I waited, pent up, in the most distressing frame of mind, for the bellow of the 'find'. But he reappeared looking perplexed, carrying chairs; and all the time I had no idea where Pietro was, and, of course, dared not look. We settled nervously round the table; and I am sure the crafty women detected something suspiciously wrong in my distracted answers and spasmodic actions. They produced parcels of food and drink for the 'Merenda', Italian tea; and, even in my alarmed state of mental squitters, I was amazed at the quantity and variety of it; and dreaded to think how long it would take to polish it off. The only minute glimmer of salvation, through that racking, tittle-tattling ordeal: no condemned man, waiting for the knife to drop, to sever his head from his body, suffered acuter pangs; was the need to fetch Colm from school at four o'clock. But as the time drew gaspingly on, and the merenda was still in touch-and-go swing, one of the smart provincial ladies suggested that it would not matter being half an hour late: that the Sisters would look after him; and I dared not protest for fear of seeming in too much of a hurry. By sipping and nibbling degrees they ate the last olive, started to smoke, dregged the Aleatico, sweet red wine of the country. Confusedly I jumbled the things together, threw chairs into the house, made a senseless clatter; and breathlessly locked the door.

I couldn't believe I was on my own two feet again, tearing down the mountain, to meet Colm: the joy of release was delirious, but I still had the plump 'skeleton in the cupboard', to contend with. So I hurried back as fast as I could with Colm, to see, was he there, or was he not. When I got back to that house of terror and unlocked the door again: *there* he was; as cool and collected as a glasshouse of cucumbers, lounging in the one and only deck chair, listening to the radio. My indignation evaporated, and I started to laugh feebly with relief. 'But where were you?' He told me he had lain for three quarters of an hour under the bed, on the stone floor, listening to us talk and eat; and when The Church scoured the room, and bent to pick up his fallen pen, he admitted his heart had gone 'pit, pat, pit, pat,' which was a revelation of a heart for him.

This musical-comedy, bedroom farce episode, was not at all pleasing to my life of monastic retirement and as I intended, divine contemplation. It gave me a serious turn, fatally endangering my relations with The Church, and having some dirty repercussions later on, where Joseph was concerned. It took a ramification of acting daft bafflement for me to wriggle myself out of those. When Joseph was proud and reproving, there was nothing to touch him; he was more fearful than The Church, because I cared more for him; and I thought, this time I have gone too far, and, through my stupidity, lost him for good.

Later on, in the town, I saw Pietro and Joseph together, furiously talking; as they talk furiously in Italy, over trifles which in England would at most cause a grunt, it did not necessarily mean the floundering of my cockleshell boat; but the prospect before me looked hazardous. Pietro, in his inimitable manner, faded out; and I was left to tackle the rock Joseph; who finally told me that Pietro had spun a very creditable yarn, based on that suggestive boudoir scene heretofore related; but embroidered with some choice additions of his own. That he had brought me a bottle of cognac: there *was* a bottle of cognac from which I had offered Joseph a glass; and after drinking five each: it was a clever touch saying the number; he had made love to me, and I don't know what flagrancies of taste. It was one of those near-truth, could-have-happened, cunningly fabricated tales, that made anything I might say in defence, merely a confirmation of my faithlessness. Joseph listened to my vain ungrammatical protestations, only half understanding; then

96

looking at me, with youthful contempt, said haltingly: 'I no love liars.'

I was having a tossed-about rough passage between these two rigidly upright men—The Church, who had painstakingly looked up the word 'disillusion', to show what he thought of me; he was always looking up words to show the extent of my 'fall from grace'; and Joseph, who, knowing nothing, was sure of everything, most of all himself, and the absolute rightness of his ideas, implanted since birth. I think he was mostly right too; but it never occurs to these 'right' people, that knowing right, they could wilfully do wrong; just as, having established, for instance, that drink is bad for the stomach at certain times, they would no more think of taking it than flying without wings. That is what I am doing all the time: launching out brazenly, an unbalanced mechanism, with no idea where it will land. And not caring terribly either.

If I seem to have given too much importance to my piddling, mock, frivolous affairs, it is not that I think they are important, but that, to live at all, it is necessary to have the illusion of something going on. They were but fly spots in the dense mesh of the day; but at night it is important for me to dream that I am looking forward to meeting somebody tomorrow. I am really not awfully good at being the serene hermit, which has become my wished-on-me rôle; and I am not awfully good at meeting people either, unless pumped up with drink. I do everything to excess, as though for the first and last time; and nothing teaches me to modulate, to moderate: that there is a morning; always a ghastly awakening.

Then the wind came, and the burning passions of the hunt were blown clean away. It was not an ordinary wind, but a searing, demented thing, with a biting will of its own that penetrated to the cringing marrow of the

nethermost embedded bone. There is nothing love likes
less than the cold; and this wind was a slaying anathema
to it; shrivelling to its tender roots, the hothouse bloom.
For the next few days it was killing to be out of bed;
shivering miserably in that whistling, rattling cave: the
hotel bedroom. Sitting, stiffened with resistance, at my
washstand desk, in my only two pairs of bedsocks, and
two sweaters, with a ridiculous flowery dirndl skirt in
between. And not a blessed nook, cranny, or hole, with a
fire, to sit by. For the first time I thought seriously of
going home, for the sole reason of keeping warm; and
telegrams flew through my head. But being always slow
to act, though headstrong in action; I waited super-
stitiously for a sign, a symbol, a portent in the sky, to tell
me what to do: without which, of course, it was im-
impossible to move. None forthcoming, I hung frigidly on.

In the meantime Colm folded up with sickness and
exhaustion, and simply perishing with the unrelieved
cold. I started to get very angry and indignant at the
lack of alleviating amenities; I had still not had a waft
of a hot bath; in fact, there was no such basic article;
and bathing in the sea was now too blistering even for
me. All my family furies were awakened at the threat to
Colm, and I stormed impotently at The Church; but it
got me nowhere. There was nothing for it but for us
both to go to bed and stay there, which we did. After
two days of stench, stupefying wine, and stagnation, flat
on my back, I felt like an overstuffed, drunken taxi-
dermist's bird. But thank God: since the Pietro escape I
believed implicitly in Him: (I was, by nature, a great
believer, but could never make up my mind to discard
one God in favour of another, as they all seemed to me so
highly probable: I could see the stern fingers of in-
numerable Gods, chastising me, but not one would
beckon to me); the weather eased up, and I was never so

pleased to see a downpour of rain. I felt like a fish, thrown back in the water, after gasping on dry land: in my natural element again.

I got Colm back to school, improved after his rest, and keen, no wonder, to get out. While I rushed into the 'Campagna' as though it was the first day of Creation; I was in such a hurry to get away from our congealed mummification. It looked just made, with the earth steaming hotly, after the rain, the grasses stretching, the leaves tingling, and the new air breathing and pulsing through stalk and stem. But when I got to the house my spirits fizzled out, at the sight of yesterweek's leavings; and the prospect of blank hours in front of me, frozen at the table; till it was time to fetch Colm again.

My brain worked better and was clearer among noise and jumble; it wilted and shrank at vistas of space yawning ahead. The small outside things that were happening to me here seemed to have precious little to do with me: seeking, searching, and not all that time left to seek or to search in; for, I did not know what. So, when The Church got so wild over my slight detractions from his holy conventional code; which nevertheless, did not stop him from betraying his sacred wife, whenever the opportunity offered; it was the old, old story, not of right and wrong, but of what is seen, and what is not seen; I felt straightforward envy that he could feel so strongly about, and take so seriously my breaches of his etiquette. As though it mattered all that copulating much who lay with whom: with the black hole grinning up at the comical bodies. People have a blessed natural gift for ignoring that unappetizing, but equally un- deniable truth. But I never do, and nor did Dylan; and, since he has proved it, I forget it less than ever.

The Church's latest aberration had been to call round at the house, when Colm, Joseph and I, were locked in,

99

shivering over a squalid cup of tea made in a tin jug. To creep stealthily round the blustering wind-shaken terrace, without letting us know he was there, and pile up against the door, chairs, tables, boxes, anything heavy, to stop us getting out. It was a queer feeling, later, in the half dark, battling through the ghostly barrage. Another day he banged, and barged in, looking disappointed not to find us incriminatingly disarrayed; but, undaunted, turned on poor, awkward, harmless Joseph, and called him, in a passion of rage, all the flowery rogues and scoundrels, so much worse in Italian, he could, most effectively, lay his lascivious tongue to; reserving for me his favourite insult: Strumpet! More meanly still, than any abuse he hurled at random; he forbade me, unconditionally, to have *anybody* in the house, or he would take it straight away from me; which cornered me very prettily. He went so far as to tackle the Englishman, explaining the disgraceful situation to him, and asking for his moral support: to talk to me, as a fellow countryman, and make me see the unseemliness of my ways, and the seemliness of his, The Church's dictates. The truth of the matter was, he had never been crossed in his life before, and I was a maddening constellation of red rags flapping and waving, just out of his reach. The Englishman, though a type such classy miles away from me, had never been so close, as on this occasion: his reaction was wry amusement and, probing for the cause of so exaggerated a wrath over so small an incident, a dry reference to 'The green eyes of the little yellow God' . . . that cause such havoc to the stablest, ordinarily pillars-of-rectitude, doubly falling, people.

I felt bad about the Englishman, having typed him as that unapproachable breed: the pugnacious Public School man, *and* Scotch, than which no other is more limited, dogmatic, or, as a rule, further from the point. Greatly against my romantic will, which gave the Italians graceful preference over my own crabbed kind, I had to admit he was the only person I could have anything approaching a conversation with; and though his jokes were of a very prehistoric, juvenile smut order, at least he made a noble attempt at fun. The Italians were not only abysmally deficient in it; but they had never heard of the absurdity, and gazed, with pitying incomprehension, should anyone *not* say precisely what they meant. In my old world of excess of verbal fun-making, I used to scoff at it, and did not appreciate how much it mattered as an underlying ingredient.

When the Englishman announced one night with jubilant elation, that he was off to England in a few days and was staying over Christmas, and perhaps longer: 'Was I going back the same time, and could we travel together?' I felt a lurching twist of longing in my guts, to be rid of this artificial show I was amateurishly producing, with me, as the bolstered-up Dame, clowning all the scenes; to wallow in baths, hot water bottles, and anonymous nannies. The thought of losing the last 'crust' of rugged turf was devastating to me; as departing people do, we developed a sudden panic affection for each other.

Then came the real show-down with The Church; my drooping flags of independence taunting him, he was marching to a foregone victory. His next move was drastic, after a thunderous Sunday. There was a farewell lunch, with me acting hostess, a job I was hopeless at, to the Englishman and the retired Colonel, with his wife and three children. Not sparkling company; they sat, tensed, silent, spellbound, listening uncomprehendingly, to the Englishman, and my mumbled, rumbled comments; swooping vulture swift over their plates, which to my horror I saw were insufficiently filled: a bit of spite on the part of The Church as I was out of favour. I recalled the lunch they had given me in their house: which was just the one room with the beds, and their all in it, lace-clothed for the occasion, with the kitchen, a stable at the bottom of the path, from which a six course meal was carted up and down: Antipasto, pasta, pesce, carne, frutta, formaggio; all cooked by the Colonel. Then, as the last damnably unpopular touch, to our heavy-going mute unorganized lunch, Joseph joined us at the table.

I asked for a glass for him, which The Church put as far away as possible; and poured with consummate loathing, averting his dignified head, a trickle of wine into. The wretched boy had gone and dolled himself up in his Sunday best, and, for the first time, looked raw and unprepossessing; I could not believe such a grotesque transformation had taken place: stiff cardboard, brand new, jerkin, zipped uncompromisingly up to the chin, zips on pockets to match, glaring almost orange trousers, black patent-leather pointed shoes. Where was my beautiful Joseph with his eternal sweater of navy blue stars, his earth-dulled working trousers, his soft boots; used by everybody on the shelving stones of this country, including me, when all my other shoes had gone to shavings. But *he* was not at all cast down by his spivvy appearance; on the contrary, he was cockily delighted with himself, thought he looked lovely, which was an added offence to me. I despaired: can love be snuffed out so quickly, at the mere change of outer raiment? After a few too many drinks for his unaccustomed constitution, he normally drank nothing, he asked me to come out walking with him; and like a mesmerized sheep I went. That was the turning point in The Church's patience, and caused his drastic move.

As I was returning in the evening; there he was; and if

ever the gates of salvation were closed on me, they were padlocked now; his whole enormous frame, with bowed legs set square, and featureless physiognomy, was padlocked. He asked me, with clipped formality, for the keys of my house, said the proprietor would come to see me tonight, and would I get ready to leave for London tomorrow. He did not want me in his Albergo, giving it a bad name, any more. It was no use me pretending I was not shaken, and in terror-struck doubt that this time I would not be able to break down the immense cliff of his towering righteousness. I said nothing then, just ran past him, head hanging, up the stairs. But I could see now that cat-cunning tactics on my part, were very necessary; stumbling words were useless at this dramatic stage if I was to accomplish anything to my profit. The only two effective props at my ignominious disposal were: the dubious advantage that I was a woman, which I was apt to forget myself at times, but which I must lay on thick as cheese spread, with a battleship shovel; using all the ancient weapons of tears, hysterias, destitution in a foreign land, weak, abandoned, no one in the world but him; and, hardest of all for me, pleading brokenly on my bended knees. The other weapon, which I was even more reluctant to use, since it was closer and more true to me, was my cossetted sorrow. But it had got to be done to explain my indifference to what I did, or what happened to me; the to him unnatural lust to do damage to myself; though he was incapable of understanding such a fatalistic attitude.

So, after supper; which for the first time we did not go to the kitchen to choose, but had it slammed down rudely in front of us; when I had put Colm to bed, he came to the room, and told me the proprietor was waiting outside. Not, I swear, the proprietor at all, but a relative; they are all related, as usual, in these small towns; living in a house on the opposite mountain, higher than, and looking straight down into mine. So that he could plainly see, and what he could not see he could make up, all the comings and goings. He had, as plainly to me, been rustled up by The Church, to give authenticity to his threat.

By then I was in a fair state of nerves myself, having been steeling myself, with nips of *caffè corretto* courage, for the interview. I swept in, in my grand manner: the distinguished foreign visitor that moment stepped off the boat, with no idea in the world what all the fuss was about. The stooge proprietor looked even more abject at being put in such an embarrassing corner than I dared to hope; but, with a conspiratorial nod of encouragement from The Church, he started to gabble incoherently about the streams of young men he had observed one after the other visiting the house. It was strange I had not observed them on my long lonely vigils; it must have been as good as the pictures, pinned to his window day and night, like a punctured moth. What was he complaining about? and didn't he have any work to do? Then, with a truly loathsome gesture, he put his tongue out, a good six wet inches, toothless as well; and tapped the tip knowingly, with his greasy finger, to indicate that people were talking. I refrained from saying people always talk, and how lucky for them to have something to talk about: my 'house of ill fame' was as good a topic as any. I was beginning to believe in it myself, but I did deserve a rake-off from all the fun and games.

My indignation was gently rising, as between the two of them, all in my own interests of course, they poisonously manufactured this scapegoat of myself. Suddenly, without adequate words to defend myself, they came: the tears that I was afraid would not materialize, they not only came, but I could not stop them. Frustrated beyond all endurance I refused to pick up, or clink glasses with these two mischief-making men, some achievement for me; made a bolt for the bedroom, and slammed the door. Childish, I agree, but gratifyingly effective. I sat trembling on the bed, with the recollective spasms I thought I had lost, getting a galvanized grip on me again; listening with the detached ear, for the *sotto voce* continuation in the next room. I could hear muffled shuffling, urgent whispering, click of lights out; and an instant later The Church was with me; bringing my wine, in chastened servitude, with an almost human look on his face. He said at once that he would not take the key as long as I promised to stick to his conditions, and gave up speaking to, or having anything to do with Joseph, or any of the *giovani*; and, for propriety's face, nobody must go to the house excepting him. He would be pleased to keep me in his hotel, do everything he could for me, so long as I behaved with more decorum, as a decent woman should. He had evidently given the brush-off to the stage proprietor at very short notice.

I had heard all this pontificating, many in-one-ear-and-out-the-others before; but when he brought out my letters, treasured by him; and showed how much they, and I, meant to him; I was moved to compassion at my capricious treatment of him. If it truly was love; but I had stopped believing in that old thing; all his flights of violence were dearly pardonable. Was he not right, come to that? I had no choice in any case, so I promised.

Life in Rio, without The Church's approbation, was as prohibitive as a death sentence; there would have been no alternative but to leave, and I did not want to leave yet, not because I was having a good time, the diametrical reverse, but because, when I got terrible pangs of yearning for my own, somebody to tell things to, to hold on to; somebody who understood my awfulnesses; I had to tell myself scathingly that I had nothing, and nobody, and would I kindly shut up. I know I had the other two children, and I loved them, and wanted very badly to see them; but children are children for all that, and come under a separately aloof heading. They should never be used as washing lines on which to hang out the clinging smalls of affection. Greater love hath no mother than to leave them alone. And, since recapitulating The Church's impetuous actions, in the light of his hotly-denied love for me; they became immediately, vastly more sympathetic, and I set a perceptibly higher value on him: so much for the whipped cream of flattery.

All the same, this new régime he imposed on me, of reinforced exclusiveness, did not leave me a wide range of distractions; since the cafés, and public drinking were out of bounds. A bottle in the house, yes; or a glass in the hotel: meaning no other than that cheerful hotel bedroom, where I had spent so many gnawing, digging deep into the pit of reminiscence hours; trying to summon the courage of will to move, to get out, and to face those strangers' appraising, animal stares. Since the Englishman and his wife had packed up on me, and the classy ladies now kept a safe distance from me, it left me solely the retired Colonel: a very old, very small man, submerged to his bushy eyebrows in his beard, who never spoke to me, but rapped out sharp orders into military vacancy. As for The Church himself, the most I ever got out of him was a snatched coffee or tea; not that he was mean, but he did not drink at the *wrong* hours: I could never discover the right ones. I scarcely saw him at all, except when he brought our breakfast early in the morning; and might or might not, I used to pray *not*, roll me on the bed, in a matter of seconds. Then off to his Municipal office, where in a posh vault of a room: with an almost invisible dark secretary in one corner; he put on his most important face, and tapped, and dictated, and referred back to, on secret official business, till two o'clock. But I did not see him again till I returned, from my frigid gestations, in the evening; nevertheless, if I happened to be wandering up and down the streets, killing time till we could eat, and stopped to talk to someone; he was always just behind me, ready to usher me on. He allowed me one black coffee—surreptitiously laced with cognac by friendly Massimo, the bar boy—after dinner. To make clear his devilish intentions to me, he nodded, winked, heaved his enormous shoulders, and stealthily disappeared; five minutes later, with long-suffering forbearance, I joined him, lingered as long as possible, over the indispensable dictionary, hoping he would leave me to my own devices; but he never failed to see me safely up the stairs first.

But I could not forget there was Joseph to be considered, who knew nothing about these new stringent measures, and who had regained all his weekday charm, with his early rising hacking work, and familiar old, loving clothes. How was I going to tell him? In the end I composed a letter in, as near as I could get to baby English; though I was never good at expressing myself simply; trying to explain to him my difficult position. But to take the sting out of: 'I must not see him any more,' I added that I loved him still, and perhaps later . . . So reluctant is love to part with any part of itself. Or should I say so tenacious is a bitch of her carrion meat.

Joseph, far from being disheartened by my letter, was bouncier than he'd been for a long time, and I had a tough job persuading him that it was serious. He refused to understand a word that I was saying: and I did feel a daft cow, a free woman of my age, with three children, explaining that I was not allowed even to speak to him in the street, by a mad landlord, who acted, with no right in the world over me, more proprietarily than a jealous husband. Joseph just laughed at me, and wanted to know why I listened to Mussolini, as he called The Church; why didn't I leave the hotel, go somewhere else, do what I wanted, and take no notice of The Church, and his determination to lock me in a box. Life is only as simple as that to the very young; and I wondered why I didn't; if nothing else there was always the unpaid bill to be considered: one of the unpleasant mundanities that took precedence over my waxing and waning romances. But I could not expect Joseph to understand that; or that it was in the realms of possibility to like, while rebelling against, and getting indignant with, the bully who wielded such an unjust, exterminating rod. I was, in truth, torn between disgust at his gross presumption and touched at the sweetness of him bothering at all with me, especially so rageously. Nothing was worse, I discovered, than being cast off altogether, and being given the awful impersonal over-effusive; as everything was over-effusive with him, politeness; of a total, hard, uncaring stranger.

X

THE sea ought to have been azure blue, and as smooth as a mill pond: has anybody ever seen a mill pond? but it was angry and grey, wave curling and snarling, and red at the edges, with iron dust in its eyes. The boats sat patiently, in their harbour ranks, as boats do, only once in a very special, mild, ecstatic while, being disturbed to shiver the water. I am not implicating the stout, black, housewife steamers, trundling up and down, to the far breakneck pier, and on to the mainland, and back; pulling behind them giant lazy tugs of the inescapable piled-up mineral cargo. The sleep-by-day fishing boats could be seen at night, with their lights, peering through a glass-bottomed tubular contraption, used to scour the tantalizing, magnified, elusive, weed-wonderful underwater world, for fish. So blasé and cosmopolitan, that she had the slenderest and briefest of connections with Rio, the svelte passenger steamer called twice daily, from the mainland: once at eight o'clock in the morning, and once at five-thirty in the evening. This was the big occasion of the day, when every social-minded person went down to meet her, and we never missed if we could help it, eagerly scanning the faces of the distant arrivals. I do not know who we hoped to see, but it was impossible not to hope. She would not lower herself by coming too close, she waited well outside the harbour for the boats to row out for her passengers; and, as soon as she had dropped them, she speeded blithely away, all her lights blazing, to some more reputable port.

Even this surely blameless diversion, which I said was for Colm's sake, but which was actually as big a thrill for me: the nostalgia of departure, while knowing we were not allowed to depart yet, had nowhere, or nobody to depart to; just to breathe the atmosphere of movement and change was invigorating, all by itself: a sucked transparent acid drop, of that end-of-term devouring frenzy, to return to those strangling aprons, and strings and pins, we fought so hard to break; or a prisoner's wild delight at a blade of grass, pushing bravely through the stones, a live mouse, a flying bird lurching against the bars, a postage stamp of sky—yet even this second-hand, mostly imaginary pleasure, was disapproved of by The Church. I don't know what Bacchanalian rapes he envisaged at the end of that grim, windswept, pier pointing to eternity; but sooner or later, on urgent, raincoated, skull-capped business, he would come striding down, searching keenly to right and left, and when he saw us huddled together against the wall, would ostentatiously look away, talk importantly to friends, give us one more cuttingly despairing glance, as though we had already sold body and soul on a public market; and go back to his kitchen, where God reigned.

One of God's chosen symbols was his television set, which he invited me to watch, whenever I wanted to. I was already prejudiced against it, having suffered the holy rites in Wales of this sacred mahogany elephant: nobody was allowed to speak, move, or drink, while being buried alive with documentary plebeianaries; people are paid to do these irksome jobs, so why should we pay to see them do them; parlour games treated like Bach Chorales; and almost everything else, on ice. Without the ice to tingle my spine I should still be sitting, a wedge of solidified rice-pudding viewing, till Purgatory come. But God's set bore no resemblance to this slick, light entertainment: an Operetta was announced in the paper, but nothing at all appeared on the screen. There was a deafening roar, jags of child's lightning, darting crazily up and down, vibrating through the set, the room, and the immobilized company. Instead of turning the thing off, they solemnly, again with no irreverent refreshment, sat through the whole blank Operetta; merely remarking at the end that the reception was not very good owing to atmospheric disturbances; but, notwithstanding disappearances, nothing out of the ordinary.

The most recent of my numberless 'new lives' was suffering a certain laxity in the efficiency of its rules, owing to two unexpected Feast days, for no reason that I could tell, stopping all work, and loosing Joseph, to put me in a dilemma. It was next to impossible not to talk to him, and too puerile not to walk up the street with him; we were nearly back to where we were, except for the loving; but it was an insuperable except; The Church had seen to that, and we were both edgy and temperamental. How much unnecessary anguish is undergone for the lack of a private place to lie down; Dylan and I would often pity the courting couples in the winter.

Not only are men unimportant when the sun shines, they are an encumbrance and a nuisance; my ruling wish is to be rid of them for evermore, to let the sun fill me, insinuate itself subtly into every hidden part of me, roast my entrails, dazzle and delight the shape of me; but it was a deceptive winter sun, with all the buzzing sleepiness of going on for ever. Every minute out of it was a crime, so when I had laboriously performed my morning ritual, I snatched up my bathing suit and towel, and started down the zig-zag path to the sea, treading on hallowed ground, consecrated to me alone. But being me, I couldn't go to the safe bay I knew, but had to dare myself to go a step further, to the next, rocky precipitous one: where the water swirled and fumed in green ecstasy against the rocks, and I gazed fascinated, longing and afraid.

When the moment of immersion was upon me, I made every excuse to prove to myself that it was not necessary, knowing all the time that it had to be done: that it was one of the prices I had to pay for my over-indulgences. When at last I plunged my body in, and it rolled with the changing waves, the water was so strong, I could not feel it at all: I had a delicious sense of triumphant disembodiment. Now I was truly prepared to conquer the world, another of my childhood boasts; all the 'trials by ordeal' in the hotel bedroom, in the searing wind, the down-pouring rain, the rattling paralysis of my house with the constant boom of a faulty radio jabbering French in-anities, were washed tempestuously away. Not content with my victory over these advancing armies and battalions of waters, I must seek fresh perils; clamber-ing over more gigantic rocks, round the foot of the cliff, back to my original bay; where I dipped again, and defied the plunging elements. But did I feel good afterwards, when I got back to my clothes, which I was in danger of losing for ever; and did the wine, at my house, taste twice as good, with the virtue of achievement.

This state of sublime grace lasted till nearly four o'clock, when it started to get chilly, and I had to fetch Colm. I could feel a gradual unpleasant sinking of elation, and the niggling realities beginning to take possession again. But, I told myself, to have possessed, even for a short time, those uplifted sensations, should be sufficient; to know that they are there, and can be experienced, should make me grateful. All the flat, pedestrian time in between, I should be content to live on that last experience; and be working towards the next revelation, whenever it should see fit to come. My fault was that I expected the permanent discoloured stream of life to be on that same high, vivid, inspired level, which was obviously; even to an advanced mystic, not practical.

It occurred to me, I had neglected badly my mysticism lately, which I used so devoutly to seek: transported on a cloud of Russian candles, jangling incense, and penetrating, deep male, high female, incanting, lowing, moaning, lacerating voices. . . . I was theirs, if they would but take me, down to the lowliest toenail. Segregated in severe, Jewish Fathering tabernacles; prostrated, more absolutely, at the wonderful ceremony of the Mass, at its best: I know that it is wrong to discriminate, a religious snobbery, that a true believer feels the same whatever the quality of the ceremony. To me it is a great work of art, and something more, so that when it is vulgarized, tinselled, made a cheap pantomime, as in Ireland, it does nothing but make me angry. But when it is austerely done, in remote cathedral unhumanness, the Latin mysterious and clear, the male chant, and answers, poignantly impersonal, inevitable, touching a starved tract of virgin emotion; the timeless vestments that take the sting out of man, the extraordinary beauty of the hands making a symbolic Jesus gesture: I can never understand why the simple parting of the hands, holding them sideways and upright, in the traditional benedictory posture, should be so indescribably moving; is as near as humans can get to expressing the divine in themselves.

So I decided, on the celebration of the Madonna, to have another look in the church, to see if I could recapture one little particle of that magic. With elaborate preparation, and agonized squeezing, I got myself into my black, which I knew was a sure winner, and made me popular with everybody; even The Church complimented me on my chic correctitude of attire. But I could not get over my own aversion to black, and I only put it on to please people, which for some obscure, putting-me-in-my-place reason, it always did; but the inner, boiling-over me, felt all wrong. So off I went with the Colonel's wife, Colm, and a borrowed fichu over my head. For quite some time I was too conscious of myself, the curious looks, and the café cognacs trundling up and down the too confined space: I wondered if I was going to faint, my speciality in the torpor of stuffy, school, Protestant churches; to notice very much. There was nothing impressive about it: a shiny gilt altar, with candles with electric bulbs in them, one of the worst innovations, a pallid, insipid, simpering virgin in the middle; and below a young, plump priest, preaching as though his life depended upon it, which I suppose it did, in a cracked voice that cared nothing for the sense of what he was saying: he had said it all so *many* times before, and it had been dinned in for so long.

All I could think of, while looking at his beautiful face, moving it seemed, with none of his own volition; and his very well-fed and tended body: how I wished for a flowing garb like his, to spread myself in; was paint. There was nothing else to do with these people, who were permanently posing for their portraits, whether there was anybody there or not to paint them: instinctively I reached for my oils. From the nun in charge of the spasmodically wriggling, punching each other, one minute quiet as reverent mice, the next effervescent as hopping mad grasshoppers, mixed bag of boys.

Once again, I was confronted with the baffling problem of how to paint white on white: the chalky white of her carved face, framed by the inside white of her coif, prolonged by the uncompromising white of her starched bib; and all the rest black, blackest black; except for the white hands, fingering the beads dribbling from the black crucifix: the white lips whispering to Him. To the kneeling old, layered in cracking paint, bent and shaking, like bad Shylocks, posed, in rigid humility, at the frilly altar rail, eyes closed, tongues out, thirsting for the taste of the magical wafer: the transforming body of Christ.

But no magic came to me: it was always difficult for me to relate the tawdriness of the props with the unquestioning faith of the people; and unless the ceremony rose, through music, to a more spiritual level, I was left cold-slabbed and abandoned, on the bank, while the faithful sailed happily into heavenly pasturing waters. I was only grateful that Colm had sat, rapt as a painted angel, through all the haranguing, and, at the end, complained bitterly that it was over, that it had been too short; and there was I dying to get into the air.

Talking of angels reminds me of the most inaptly named man in Rio: poor Angelo. He was either born with, or had suffered a ghastly disfigurement; his whole face was as if turned, with one deft movement, inside out: a torn chunk of bulbous, pitted, bleeding raw meat. My 'look at everything, be afraid to look at nothing' principle was painfully tried, looking at him. But one of the nice things about the Italians was their perfectly natural acceptance of Angelo, as though there was nothing out of the ordinary about him, and he was intimately like one of them. Not only Angelo, but all the other oddities, freaks of nature, grotesques: the indispensable idiot, in every small town, simmering with inbreeding and incest. This one, an overgrown, ageless girl, pigtailed and bucket mouthed, who slouched and gaped, swept up imaginary dirt, browsed intently in books, and appeared to be a permanent resident in Colm's school. The fantastically twisted and knotted, with all the hideous swollen joints of locked rheumatism. The corkscrew of a man wheeled out, with no sense of 'there are certain things better not seen'; a cigarette pushed, haphazard, into his sideways-slipping mouth, which he had to lean over backwards to hold on to, like a broken bird impaled over a barbed-wire fence. His hands spoke for themselves: they grappled uselessly on his shrivelled knees, asking in the queer, disconnected with the possessor, brazen display, common to the infirm and deformed: to be taken notice of. And the dogs and the cats, whom they treat with much the same brutal tolerance: what a verminous crew they are. Although I am no more partial to them enthroned in palatial eminence, as in some other besotted English-speaking countries. Here they are not exterminated, I wish they were, but they are not fed either, so they are as ravenous, as skulking, as scavenging, as any self-respecting rat; and I had an overpowering revulsion, if they came anywhere near me. At night I could hear outside, the harpy, excruciating yowling of those amorously dissolute cats, which was quite enough to put me off the romantic contemplation of 'love' for a long miaouling time.

Slovenly the Madonna's day dragged on: once I have dressed up, with stockings and high-heeled shoes, there is not a hope of me doing anything sensible till I change back into country rags. There was no alternative but to join the rest of the crowd, interminably fashion-parading, up and down the old familiar main street. At four there was a procession for the Madonna: she was borne aloft, the same sad figure, looking pathetically exposed, and in need of a good warm overcoat; or perhaps it was just us, freezing to death following her. The handsome priest again, capaciously wrapped and draped, more mellow than ever, with his skinny, angular serving boys, leaping round him. The brass band blaring out, most unsuitable popular songs, in the rear. It came to a halt in the main square, to hear the Pope's blessing squeaked out of a scraping amplified radio.

It certainly was a day, one of those that seemed like never finishing: when nothing will come soon enough. I started drinking all the wrong things at the wrong times: wine at tea time, tea at aperitif time, with an aperitif straight after, and dribs and drabs of this and that, of which I lost count in the maze of Madonnas, marching to and fro, and caterwauling voices. But I was simply not strong-minded enough to sit, as they did, at a table, with nothing in front of them, by the hour, talking vociferously, or not talking at all: just gazing placidly, the thing they were best at, as though they could never see enough, and had all the time in creation.

We passed The Church in an enormous cowboy hat, strangely shrunk, in his posh, pressed, neutralizing clothes; but all affability until, as inevitably happened, Joseph materialized, as though drawn by a magnet. Whereupon The Church turned smartly on his heels, and briskly: putting as much expression into the irate beat of his steps as though he had spat in my eye and had done; walked in the opposite direction.

Now Joseph was becoming a serious menace; I don't mean a menace in himself, because I could never stop myself smiling as soon as I saw him; but a serious menace to my feelings. He was the first person who had got anywhere near me since Dylan; only because he had bombarded his way in, like a clumsy, but very seductive, and equally callous child. Those wonderful whirlpools of dankly greasy, black grass hair, that it was an insult to the Creator not to fondle; the untypical greenish, far-away eyes; the peace and calm of his spreading shoulders;

the breadth and hardness of his thighs in their tight trousers; the superb effrontery of his youth, and moral rectitude; the principles he still believed in, and would expound to me, like a new flaming Ten Commandments; made him very difficult to resist or deceive. The last thing I wanted was a deep emotional disturbance; and least of all from a stripling of his age. As long as I held the reins, I didn't care how many horses I had to drive, but once the reins were taken out of my hands, and I lost control: then the prospect began to look not so healthy for me. Because I was mortally afraid of this one indignity, and determined he should not suspect the depth of my feelings, I went to absurd manipulations to prove to him that I was an unredeemable drunkard, shallow, frivolous, and prepared to make love to any man. All of which could be conclusively proved by my standing at the café bar, with a glass of wine, talking to a man. But, in the meantime I got no love of any description, corporeal or spiritual.

One discordant Sunday we were out walking in the morning, Colm, me, and Joseph, casual and ordinary, with a tang of family glum habit; when we met, at a bend in the country road, a group of sportsmen with guns, resting. Joseph started fooling with a gun, and shooting at a paper he had fixed on a stone some distance away; then, still fooling, he offered the gun to me, never expecting me to take it, as he had very fixed ideas as to the weakness and limitations of women: similar to Dylan, with his bed and kitchen. Little he knew what he did: as soon as I felt the gun in my hands, I had a trembling lust to kill, to commit a violence, an explosion of that too placid, taken for granted, pastoral scene; caring nothing for me, and my Dylan-smouldering cracked volcano. I held tight to myself, and to the gun, concentrating on Colm, to save me from my nonsense; how often had he saved me before. The picture of his bafflement at the sight of my mutilated body, and the diminutive, curly figure, toddling to nobody, or anybody, was too gruesome, even for my, as I thought, unsentimental heart. So holding as steady as I could, I turned firmly from the provocative group, and pointed the gun, as far as I could judge with two eyes, since I could not close one, steadfastly at the paper, and fired. The shot flew up in the air and the jolt knocked me backwards; but I felt, in some infernal region, liberated, as though I had burst out of a too constricting corset.

Joseph looked at me with a new amazed respect, unable to believe I had fired the gun; bringing home to me sharply the fundamental differences between our two nations. But how delightful to be reminded that the men are the strong ones, who do all the dangerous things, must never flinch, and work to protect their feeble, fat women: if only it were possible to believe it. There was I, father and mother in one, teetering unsteadily between the two, and harbouring the double strength of both. More than Joseph, in his innocence and softnesses, could ever have had the necessity for: good, brave Joseph, but untried. Thus the little rustic party broke up: on that mountain road, in the faintly glimmering winter sun; the ruddy-faced, corded men, belted becomingly with strung bullets, assembled their shooting gear, and drove off with Colm and the dogs, all on top of each other; leaving us to follow on.

Pietro, whom I had sworn never to talk to again, after his betrayal to Joseph of his visit, in the plural with him, to the house, grossly embellished; had, nevertheless, beguiled himself back into my company, by sheer exterior sweetness, captivating French politeness, and utter lack of any moral sense, honesty, or seriousness. He was lightly refreshing after my other two high-minded guardians of my virtue; except for themselves. It never seemed to occur to either of them that if I was, or did, all the things they wished me to be, and do; or rather not do; I would be outside their scope altogether, safely tucked into a virginal garden, far away from temptation; and that included them. That their possible possession of me as a perverse plaything, was dependent upon a considerable perversity in me; and if they got rid of that, they got rid of their own distractions into the bargain. But Pietro brought me little gifts of handkerchiefs, scent, made me compliments: the others never wildly dreamed of doing that; and it was as difficult not to respond to him, as to not take a bite out of a delicious, succulent nectarine; but there was a very cankerous stone, I must not forget, inside. He was born *not* to work, and had painstakingly avoided it so far, as something beyond the realms of his fluffy chick incubation. His father had been a rich seagoing man; but, for the first time, he was pinned down to a job, inevitably connected with the mines. Impossible to visualize him rough clad, attacking with a pickaxe, along with the regular working crowd, a sheer face of rock. But, whatever he did: I tried to conjure up the Italian equivalent of a tea-boy; he had to get up at six o'clock: and that surely was a big feat for him. When I sympathized with his tribulations, he shrugged his shoulders evasively and said, *'C'est la vie.'*

I had not seen Mister, the dustman, for some time: he mostly stayed in his waterfront district, where there was a small, smelly, usually deserted, café-bar. I also frequented this tawdry shop, usually to get a bit of privacy to write cards or letters, and for these nocturnal 'out of my orbit' visits, I was severely criticized by The Church, who constantly referred to my true 'ambiente'; sounding to me like a golden ambience flatteringly surrounding me, but disappointingly turning out to be no more than my old bugbear, society. One evening I was down there with Joseph and Colm: it was the only place we could go where the vigilance was not so keen and the spies not so numerous: and as always, when we went in, Gigi, the landlord, and his wife, were still eating. It was the only occupation that was not disapproved of in Rio and had precedence over everything else. I sometimes wondered what would happen if somebody had the bad taste to die in the middle of 'mangiare': I am certain they would clean their plates religiously before attending to them. Has anybody ever seen the expression of awed reverence, touching the divine beatitude, on an Italian's face, when counting money: it is not unique to him, but with him everything is accentuated one hundred per cent. Or the manner in which he *descends*, there is no other word, like a napkin-tied, lip-licking, seam-splitting vulture, haughtily intent on his food; and, indecently teetotal on the job, using wine as a necessary, but not particularly pleasant, means to wash it down. The very reverse of the English system, where food is a rather unpleasant, but necessary, padding, eaten privately if possible, in deference to socially more important drink.

On such an eating night as this did Mister ask us to lunch on Sunday in his house. We sat in a very small room, at the back of a building, with a bed and a table in it; and his daughter aged sixteen, an English sixteen at that, which precluded her adolescently from the conversation; eating, for a change, spaghetti; with a magnum bottle of vinegar white wine in front of me, that only I, in desperation, was trying to get to the bottom of. With Colm asking gramophonically: where were the other rooms? in spite of sharp raps on the head from me. If only poor people would not always apologize for being poor; Mister was continually harping about his humble best; and put on such a show of false daintiness, that everybody was embarrassed. It always makes me feel like doing something outrageous to put them at their ease, to make them behave like natural people again, instead of living up to, like petrified puppets, the brave disguise of want. I wanted to fling my food about, spill things, make a disturbance; anything to break up the stilted artificial circle, to put some life into the stuffed dummies. As soon as Mister was out of his matchbox castle, back in the smelly familiar café, playing cards; he became his all too human self again, and it was possible to talk and joke without being paralysed by the stringent need to make a meaningless pretence.

It was Dylan's old, as usual wise, argument about keeping out of people's houses; only meet them in public places; and, even more forcibly, keep them out of yours. However rough, ready, and hospitable, there is an immediate drop in spontaneity the moment that the door of a private house closes behind you, and your friend becomes, compulsorily, your host or guest. According to Dylan houses should be kept entirely for recuperative and family purposes; according to me, it is purely a question of money: with a fleet of cooks and butlers, I think I could be a very good hostess. I have a peculiar aversion, not to working, but to being seen working, partly because I can do nothing when I am being watched, and very little when I am not; and partly because it is a hangover of the extraordinary way our mother brought us up: not only was it not done to talk about money, but also, to sully one's hands. We were taught all the appurtenances of ladies, with none of the circumstances in which to practise them. Living in the depths of the country, seeing nobody, on very little money: not that we were aware of it or anything else material or practical for that matter; in rags, running wild, reading at random, produced a very incongruous band of guerilla ladies. Result: blissfully unfitted, in every social and domestic respect, for the wifely rigours before us. But then, as our mother assiduously impressed upon us, she had prepared us to marry rich men; notwithstanding that we never had the opportunity of meeting any, and, of course, none of us did.

How did Dylan get into this again? He cropped up again in the hairdresser's, without a word of warning. I was just sitting waiting to have my hair washed, among a typical catch of teeming, shampooing, oiling, black-hair-frizzing, noisily scandalmongering women; when one of them, netted and pinned, like a monster-headed fish, under the menacingly droning, porpoise-puffing dryer, produced an old newspaper and handed it to me. There was Dylan, in a photograph I had never seen before, staring me in the face, as much as to say, 'You bloody fool, what do you think you are playing at?' The blood rushed to my face, as though I had been caught out doing something shamefully wrong; the island foundered under the sea, and all the things I had tried so hard to make seem important, and almost, at short times I thought, succeeded, went, soundlessly, with it.

So much for my dalliance with The Church's fiery tempers. So much for the burning pain of Joseph. Yet at least, let me say in my favour, I did not betray the outward symptoms of my partiality for him. I did, but he was not old enough to understand them, as I went to opposite extremes, and the Italians are very literal minded: if you say, or do, so, you mean so. Impossible for them to understand that a Britisher will do almost anything, except the thing that matters most to him. His overruling fear is the betrayal of the human heart: he will fling himself over precipices, scale pyramids, scour the heartless, snow and ice lengths of poles, for the sake of the anonymity of the human heart. Joseph was naturally intelligent, while properly understanding nothing; when I playfully called him a thief for picking up my matches by mistake, his whole countenance darkened, as only an Italian's, who uses his face as a reflection of his mind, not as a blind as we do, can; and, without a word, he walked straight out. How can you explain shades of meaning to a mentality like that? Even after hours of tongue-splitting explaining, he was not convinced; he accused me of all kinds of incredible slights to his *amour propre*, which was as blinding as the sun in his eyes: of laughing at him, thinking him stupid, when my only concern was to hide my love from him; not to stir up that still whirlpool of hair eddying from his intensely serious head. And to think that one look from a faded newspaper had given the lie to my tender fancies, my would-be romantic return to childhood; had wiped out as thoroughly, as snow wipes out a landscape, my poor protesting fabrications.

XI

JOSEPH and I had twice got ourselves, quite by chance, invited to wedding parties; and I felt pretty silly always turning up partnered by this naïve boy, who could almost have been my son; and sitting in state at the head of the table with him, as though we were the next on the list. The first one started at eight o'clock in the morning, straight after the marriage ceremony. I had forgotten all about the invitation, from Mario, a jolly, rollicking, seafaring man: one of the rarities who drank wine in tumblers, before *and* after eating, and had the temerity to get visibly tipsy, to The Church's unbridled contumely. So Joseph waited in the street, below my window, three hours for me, till I strolled down, innocent as hell, at eleven o'clock. We got there just at the tail end, when most of the guests had had their fill and gone, and only the stragglers and tipplers and out-of-hand children, festooned themselves, idly replete, about the long littered table. The newlyweds sat rigidly, silently, eyes lowered, holding hands; he, as if he once lifted those heavy bed-dreaming lids, would be lost in voluptuous drowning; she, as meek with acceptance as a hypnotized lamb, waiting the thrust of the slaughterer. We offered them our best wishes, and they rose to give us their seats.

Then the customary procedure began: first, three sugared almonds put in the palms of our hands, then a heaped plate of goodies: sweets, sweet pastries, froufrous, wedding cake. It was an insult not to eat up every one, even just before lunch. Then a regiment of even sweeter, highly coloured, clogging liqueurs, drunk in swift succession. I pined for a gulp of the old acid wine, and in the end had to ask for a glass of water.

The sleep-walking pair were changing now into their impeccably-pressed, glistening with newness, tailor-mades, ready for that perilous honeymoon journey to the mainland. I could not conceive what they did there, in the winter, besides the love-making, and that has to pause for breath sometimes. Country people who normally work all day do not talk, in the conversational sense, or drink, except a glass at meals; or read as much as a newspaper, as far as I could see. It must have been one endless *passegiata*: up and down, up and down, looking into shop windows, always leisurely looking, endlessly looking, looking at each other, at nothing; with the occasional obscurity of a cinema to gather wind again. After the ritual inspection of shiny cut glass presents, glittering with pretentious cheapness, laid out with undisguised pride in the best unliveable room; which I found it hard to give the requisite exclamations of awed admiration to; we also left, stumbling and red-faced, down the stairs into the merciless street.

There was only one thing for me to do, if I was not to sicken myself for the rest of the day: fling myself sprawling into the water; so I sent Joseph, who normally never drank anything strong, and was unsteadily on the verge of actual gaiety, to collect Colm from school; and made a rush for my bay of cleansing salvation.

And then Christmas: shall I ever forget that last Christmas, or shall I ever remember it distinctly? of blurred, blunted slashing, muffled crying, submerged in rot and falsity, and all the mean dragon deceptions of the night impressions; with Dylan never so much dead, or never so much alive, in everybody's minds; with nobody saying his name; it was, willy nilly, Dylan or no Dylan, upon us again. Rather than go back to Wales, and have those same ghosts, still unlaid, rise up and slash me afresh, stinging the shrinking flesh, with their cloying grave-sodden draperies; I decided to stick it out in the stranger pit of the island. At least I can say I had a bathe on Christmas Eve, though, it must be admitted, the water was gaspingly cold to get into: I wondered if my heart would stop, but no such luck; after a few strokes it was just bearable, and I felt tingling with promises of Christ's birthday.

Going to that far bay reminded me of a not very savoury interlude, that had happened to me a little while ago, that I had tried to push into the back of my sullied mind. On my own, one day exploring farther, I was followed by a proper clot of a country oaf, more child than boy, and more animal than child; I could not tell if he was all there, or not. His lurching crouching descent, down the shelving, stone-loosening path did not at first worry me too much: but I found a foreign presence an insult to my serenity. When he kept coming doggedly on, right down into the forbidden bay itself, I felt bound to say something, to courteously hoof him out. I tried to explain, in my brutish Italian, which refused to yield the gist of my meaning, that I wanted to go in the water, and could not get undressed with anybody there. He still stood stolidly on, saying nothing. In the end I lost my temper, and started to shout at him in English and tried to push him away. Then he turned at last and slouched, ill-humouredly out of sight, and I forgot all about him.

I had just come out of the water and thrown off my suit: no visible sign of a human being in this remote inlet of uninhabited coast; and was starting to dry myself with a pocket-handkerchief sized towel, when back came the large moron lout; though obviously young he was by no means small; squatted down rudely in front of me and did no more than scrutinize. But that was enough to infuriate me caught as I was at a naked disadvantage; I was too soaking to pull on my clothes quickly over my saltily resisting body; so abandoning the useless pretence of coy modesty, with my scrap of towelling that concealed nothing; I picked up my wet suit and swung it across his face. To my mortification he only started to laugh, thought it was a game, and said: temperamental woman pleased him. This impertinence maddened me the more, and seriously worried me inside as to how I could decently escape from this ludicrous trap. Then my rage began to be mixed with fear, my fighting became more frantic; though I was still trying hopelessly to brush him lightly into extinction. I pulled some clothes on somehow: all backwards, inside out, and refusing to do up with my too strenuous, precipitated efforts; snatched my basket, and stumbled, panting, up the path.

He followed close behind me, and when we came to a small grassy clearing, hiding under my very own precious olive trees, as pure, and aromatic with sage, and lizards, and thyme, as a primitive Bible picture; he fell upon me like a hurtling tower, and I was trapped on my back, underneath him. Now, it was not even grotesquely funny: I was fighting, not for anything as dim as my honour, but for my pulsing life. Even now, only one side of me was fighting; the staid, sitting back, maiden-aunt of my mind, was saying: this is how the doomed victims of a bestial assault react, as the fingers tighten, dig deeper into the spent serpent-twitching, in the booming canal of the throat. In spite of the biting and the kicking, the fistfuls of wrenched hair, I was still half ashamed to show myself in deadly earnest of strength; and yet another voice of the devil insinuated to me: 'how much

128

easier to let him have his way.' Although he was not getting it, I was not either; we lay locked together, entangled in wanton disorder, sweating in the sun, in abortive fury. I could think of no foxy twist to break his oppressive hold on me; and though, by now, I was praying for help, at the same time I was terrified of being found so contemptibly at his mercy. Who in the logical world would believe my story? Against my inborn grain I resorted to the old dodge, and started to scream, at near hysteria strain to myself; but it also alarmed him for the safety of his own skin, and he leapt fearfully to his feet, looking guiltily surprised.

I tried hastily to gather myself, and my things together: my basket had gone rolling down the mountainside, scattering its papers and treasures dispassionately; my clothes were screwed round my waist in moist knots, and matted with straw and brambles and thorns; my face and hair fortunately I could not see, but I felt a tangled lump of tow, over flaming cheeks. Thus, in thoroughly dissolute extravaganza manner, we progressed heaving upwards. Now I understood how much I had expended, been inwardly churned up: I was twitching, perilously near to crying. But he still did not desist, made grabs: I threw his beret as far as I could over the sea, hoping his sense of property, so powerful here, would get the better of him; but for once it did not work; though I noticed he retrieved it later.

I threatened to tell his workmates, who were rebuilding a house at the top, and the police, about his outrageous behaviour, but could see by his scornful grin, he did not believe me. So when, doubly incensed, I got, dishevelled and gasping, to the house at the top; I went directly to his friends; much older, more sensible looking men; and incoherently, half in tears, blurted out my wrongs, from the importunacy of this upstart boy. But I tailed off impotently for lack of words, and seeing the pitying looks of derision they gave me. They laughed tolerantly, and said: 'Lasciare fare, é giovane'—Let him have his way, he is young. I gave up, blubbering English and Italian curses.

I fled to my house, shaking with hate and indignation against the whole Italian race. Truthfully I was more upset than I realized, and began to feel the stagnant maggots begin to hop again, and a wave of hostility swept over me. I felt a strong need to make a public protest, to assert my rights: not so much because of this one embarrassingly degrading incident, but because, if I did not, they would despise me for being so easily victimized by them; and think in future, they could treat me with the same lack of respect: as so much free dirt for all.

When The Church came to the house, I told him, while I was still distraught, the whole unpalatable story; more to keep him off the subject of my misdoings than with any unpremeditated intentions. He jumped to his feet at once, and ignoring my hesitations, led me unswervingly to the police station. He asked for the highest official, *il Commissario*, and as soon as we were seated in his private office, unstoppably poured out his highly-biassed version of my now fantasy-receding experience. I was powerless in the clutch of officialdom, nothing now could stop its half-witted purl one, slip two, plain three, and deadly stocking-stitch from thereon, course; with no, even cousin-once-removed, relationship to flesh and blood. They insisted on pinning down the minutest, and, whenever possible, the most compromising details, till I began to doubt not only myself, but the truth of my preposterous-sounding story now. It was impossible to take it seriously any more: death by strangulation or rape was far preferable to this murderous inquisition. My one and only passionate desire, at that libidinous conference, was to get out, and forget all about it; my moral righteousness had long since flown out of the barred window. But once snared in the long-winded yawning coils of the law, it is as hard to go back as it is to go forward. For the most part I simulated stupefied incomprehension, one of my specialities, which was largely genuine; not wanting to get too deeply involved in the accumulating morass, which was getting out of all sane proportions.

Then The Church left me alone with the Commissario, who turned out to be a very shrewd and likable man, not one whit affected by The Church's stern denunciation, and the weight of his importance. He raised an eyebrow and asked, was I going to sign or not? In a panic of alertness at the word 'sign', I asked, what? The petition denouncing the boy, which gave them permission to arrest him, and proceed with the law: taking it out of my hands, in fact. I carefully asked what kind of sentence this might entail for him; he obligingly leafed through a black book of crimes and penalties, contentedly humming 'Li, li, bi, bi, libi, libi;' then triumphantly '*Libidino* ah . . . eccolo!' then, after concentrated perusal, he announced, 'Anything from one to five years.'

I, who had anticipated anything from a week to ten days, was drawn up, with a jab at the bit: I knew only one thing very clearly: I must *not* sign, under pain of death. I had a cartload on my conscience already, without sending anybody to prison; I should be haunted for the rest of my miserable life. Mind you, I was thinking of myself, not him: I would have killed him with pleasure; but prison, the suffocation of the soul, No. So I shook my head, and tried to explain that I only wanted to teach him a lesson, give him a fright, so that he would not dare try his tricks again; and, from his example, stop others from taking the same liberties. The Commissario seemed to understand and sympathize with my point, told me to think it over, and tomorrow he would summon the boy to the station, confront him with me, and I could decide then what was to be done with him.

What a grim thought, but I could see there was no getting out of it now. When I got back, and told The Church about it, he was furious that I had not signed the paper there and then, and did everything under his jaundiced sun, to persuade me to do so; but, though I appeared agreeable to him, nothing could have budged me from my decision. It was *my* principles for a change, which he did not realize I possessed, and when they got into action, his petty 'Public Opinion' was all wasted on me. When I went down to the café, the retired Colonel leaned forward, and whispered conspiratorially, 'Put him in, put him in'; they could not have done more between them for me to 'Keep him out'. They represented the general public that takes such rabid delight in condemning, dissecting, and, above all, locking up.

So the next day, there I was again, sitting in that mercilessly neutral waiting-room, with the sun taunting me outside, and a very minor, plump, under-official standing in front of me: as blatantly as if he had written it in chalk on a blackboard, assessing my age, my weight, my fortune, and my purpose for gracing his select rat-trap. I was tempted to give him a clout over his smug, well-nourished, cretin's cheeks; but, on second thoughts, held my peace, for once. At last the Commissario sent for me; he was alone, playing on the typewriter as though it was a festive piano, singing out the words and punctuation, in a happy trilling stream: '. . . virgola . . . punto . . . virgola . . . punto.' Then he looked up and asked me searchingly, Had I changed my mind? I said No, but was afraid The Church did not approve of my decision; he repeated the name with a curl of his lip, amply expressing what he thought of him. But, I insisted, would he impress upon the boy the seriousness of his offence? He agreed, and sent for him.

The boy, in the meantime, had invented a cannily plausible story about me smiling at him, leading him on, coquettishly seducing an innocent babe. As he came in, all polished up, arrogant, and on the defensive, I automatically said 'Buona sera' to him, but got no answer, forgetting that it was perhaps not the thing to do, under the circumstances.

The Commissario, fixing a penetrating gaze on him, started to read my denunciation to him; he started volubly to protest, but was silenced by the Commissario, who then went on to give him such a damning, castigating, lacerating talking-to: inspired verbatim, and as lasting and sustained as an operatic aria; rounding it off with true classical repetition of the central theme: 'And it is only owing to the grace of the Signora, the grace of the Signora, that you are not this instant behind bars, awaiting trial, liable to five, to seven, to ten years . . .' He paused: 'And now shake hands with the Signora, apologize, and thank her for her gracious clemency.'

The boy turned sheepishly to me, and with surly unwillingness, shook hands, mumbled, 'grazie', and a few words under his breath, and stumbled out of the room. It was all over, I thanked the Commissario for his noble performance, and quietly retired; with the firm conviction from everybody, that I was the guilty party, since I had not done the obvious thing. I had wilfully condemned myself, but having nothing to lose, it was not a magnificent sacrifice.

I had had many opportunities of entering the padded fold of security, as now The Church was pressing me so arduously to do, and be sure to close the door behind me; and though I yearningly envied these safe comfortable people, with their lives laid out to pattern, before they opened their eyes: they had only to follow their blindly rooting noses, to reach that choiring trough of one in all, and all in oneness. Yet when it came to the final click of the latch, I stood stock still, like a frightened horse, shied convulsively, and made a bolt for the exciting perils of the unknown: which had a habit of translating themselves, more often alas, into the bed-sitter, the chandelier, and the potted palm.

XII

So concerned was The Church about all my breaches of good conduct that he went to endless pains, made long lists of my offences, and eventually summoned me to his impressive office, to read me a written lecture on the ethics of correct comportment. Here it is, translated.

I have tried many times to write, with the help of the dictionary in bad English, to express to you my disappointment (in you) for your detestable behaviour in society; but now I must, before saying good-bye and closing the parenthesis of that which is our friendship, tell you my true thoughts in Italian, in which I can express myself tolerably.

Everything you do smacks of blasphemy: I begin with the affront which you had recently from the young man.

The police have explained to me that you would not denounce or confront the youth because it was you that made him lose control of himself by your exhibition of nudity, which inflamed him to assault you in a brutal manner, to bring about an intent which he could have achieved peacefully.

This boy has declared that it was you who called him to dry you after the swim, to talk to you, and that you showed yourself to him in provocative dress, if not frankly nude. He could not therefore have behaved very differently; and if the boy had possibly been a little less impulsive he could easily have gained from you that which has been received from you by so many other young men, whom I think it superfluous to name.

I have known easy women in my day, but *None* so easily come by as you.

Even at Rio there are women who misbehave, but they do not display themselves publicly, and they know how to preserve appearances, as you do not.

At this point I warn you in your own interest, before something similar to the incident with that boy happens again, to seek a change of air because here you have a bad reputation.

That you have, until today, been able to live in this country cottage is entirely thanks to my personal interest in you; you know perfectly well that elsewhere no concessions were offered you. You have infringed the conditions imposed, that the house should not become a house of assignation—not to put too fine a point upon it. You can say that when a person takes a house, in effect he may live in it as he chooses (and you are not wrong) but if the house is given to you with certain conditions, you have no choice but to abide by the agreement.

Another very 'innocent' thing that you have done, that causes astonishment here, is that you have been seen drinking wine in public. If you have noticed, the ladies you meet in bars (not in taverns) limit themselves to coffee, tea, or liqueurs, but not wine—and if they do drink wine they do it in private, not in public; and as you see these are the anomalies which are nonetheless observable in these little country towns; while at Livorno, or in Rome it would be quite normal, I repeat that here it leads to trouble and has put you in a very bad light.

You may believe that I am very mortified to tell you this, which is in a sense a thing of no importance, habitual with you, and will certainly surprise you, but it is my bounden duty to make you understand and take count of what you have done.

Your coming was preceded by so much acclaim among our friends and I had promised myself that I would introduce you to the circle of my friends, and that this would be very good for you, and I had told everyone about you; but now I have had to take second thoughts because of the turn your visit has taken; which reached its summit that night when you, in the fumes of alcohol, took the road into the country at a late hour with that youth, and came back so much later.

All of this might have passed unobserved if your child had not fortuitously waked and gone crying into the kitchen, so that we were forced to look for you, but in vain and then since we had information that you had gone down the lane, I went after you on my Vespa, but eventually I came back because you were nowhere to be seen: and then you re-entered in a condition which you know better than I. Your clothes disarranged, and other things that showed clearly the epilogue to your walk—'innocent'!!!

You were wrong not to attend to me and to disregard my tiresome lectures, but one thing is certain. These two young men who are quarrelling for your favours are just the ones who have contributed to putting you in such a bad light in front of the whole countryside, whether through your behaviour or through gossiping of the favours bestowed upon them; and nevertheless it seems you do not intend to put an end to this state of affairs, but to keep up relations with them notwithstanding all that I have told you—

and that you continue to be the mistress of one of them and cannot tear yourself away.

You can also ask what business it is of mine, 'Am I or am I not free to lead my own life?' Of course you are—but you came here to Rio because you knew you had good and honest friends; and if you had known how to profit from their affection, which is indispensable to you, you could have been free to enjoy yourself wonderfully (it is certainly not my intention to cloister you) but now it is no longer possible, in view of your questionable relationships which have alienated you from all good company.

If you wish, you can redeem yourself and not always be the object of loose tongues—but to succeed in this, you must follow my advice, and I do not know if this will be possible for you. Have you the strength? I think not, because seriousness is not your strong point.

I forgot to tell you that among your grave faults is also that gravest that you become very loquacious when influenced by the fumes of alcohol and you recount what you have done, and with the greatest naturalness that which you intend to do, to whoever you happen to be talking with.

Of this assertion I have direct experience and I shall talk to you about it.

I conclude by saying to you that if you insist on seeing that lover of yours, who is, though it may not seem so to you, the cause of all the talk—I must absent myself from you; and my return to you is dependent on his departure from you.

All of this will seem to you absurd, but when I shall have explained to you all the reasons, you will see that I am very right.

XIII

THERE were times when these bland Italian 'children of nature' got on my nerves to such an extent that I could have murdered them for their lack of complications: this is right, and that is wrong; so we do this, and we don't do that; their calm assumption of the undulating supremacy of their unthinking bodies, unchanging customs, and brutal taboos; and their callous lack of comprehension, or even desire to comprehend, anybody not belonging, not conforming to the immemorial acceptance of things as they are, as they always have been, and as they always will be. As with a child, such egotism is sometimes winning; but there are complicating times when a coating of maturity, a picot edging of intellect are worth all the disarming children on earth. Paradoxically, when I got into a real rage with one of them, let fly, incoherently shouted at them, gesticulated, in my version of their prerogative; they began to wake up, looked at me with a new respect, and a warming bond was established; not only between us, but, like a stone dropped in still water, rippling outwards, to all around us.

Similarly, in the hotel, if I worked myself up into a frenzy of indignation about the icy conditions, no hot water, no fires, no light, quite often the current would go off for a whole day and night, and I was left padding helplessly round that eternal hotel bedroom, which had lost none of its vampire charms, and was now more bat-haunted than ever; I actually made The Church smile

139

with my fervent remonstrances. He came back loaded with hot water bottles, toddies, flower pot stoves: while the rest of the family blithely repeated, 'Niente corrente', as though that solved everything. They were always very partial to chanting, in a monotonous litany, the only too painfully obvious; old men would go about dolefully moaning, like bad actors, 'I am *old*, I am *old*, I am *old*;' respectable citizens would sonorously declare: 'I am an honest and upright man, everybody in the town respects me;' bashful youth chime in with: 'I am strong, I have great courage, I make the box with the most formidable man; I make the music, the love, the swim, the languages, the gaiety.' This idea of 'making gaiety' was also strange to my reared-on-reticence mind: it was not, with them, an effervescence that bubbled up from some mysterious spring, but a manufactured commodity as dish-water flat as the day of judgment. But then gaiety to be hilariously gay needs contrasts: it takes an Eskimo, or Russian, or all desperate Celtic peoples, to break through those snowy, choking, sun resisting walls, into a disembodied flash of sparking gaiety. And always in the background, that woman's howl that went on ceaselessly, from behind some dark unimaginable casement, 'E, O, L, O, O, O, O' as agonized as a foghorn that had had its young removed; but EOLO never went to her; and from the bottom of the town, another lugubrious voice wailed in answer: 'P, I, N, O, O, O, O,'. . . .

Christmas: try as I would to forget it, to pretend it was not there, it pressed on me like an undefinable Sunday; and with it the stinging whistle of January pierced my eardrum; and that charged air of false expectation invaded me, tell myself as I would, over and over again, that there was nothing: 'no, no, nothing, nothing no more;' at all for me to expect. Nothing but that last minute contagious fervour, that infects even the most immune agnostic stones; and that is still, in spite of the centuries of constructive disbelieving, indissoluble from the birth of Christ. More obviously so here, in this parroting Catholic nursery-rhyme book, with their *presepio* (crèche) in every house, simple or elaborate, according to their means; lovingly laid out in moist mountain moss, green herbiage, lichen from the woods; the Kings and the lambs, the shepherds bearing warm, hay sweet, fleecy coverings for the glistening bright Child; bread and wine; the ass and the bullock standing wisely by, knowing, in their animal deep understanding, they must be there; all travelling in the one direction, past the painted wooden town on the hill, the prim spotted windmill, the grey steepled church, the luminous grotto down the lit-up tunnel, the looking glass pond, the silver paper stream, towards that one big tinsel star over the glowing stable; and a solitary angel swinging, sadly on a string, above it; their parades, their masses.

On Christmas Eve there was a special Mass at midnight, to which I had promised to go with Colonel 'Beard's' wife. So I had the shivering prospect of five gaping hours of street-marching, before the appointed time. There was no such thing as a warm room to sit in, it did not to my knowledge exist in this town: they plastered themselves all over in woollen underwear, down to the wrists and the ankles, with several layers of black on top, clutched their tins of burning coals to their stomachs, and insisted that it was *sempre l'estate*, that it was always mild and beautiful here: there was no winter. They strolled serenely up and down, exactly as though it was midsummer, while I, with my flimsy nonsensicals, and all the wrong bursting clothes, had never been so cold in my life, and longed for the muggy fugs of London.

My predicament was intensified by the necessity of making a show of dressing up for the occasion: and dressing up inevitably meant taking off the comfortable bundles I had piled on at random; tearing on invisibly sheer stockings over purple bulging legs, with all the maddening suspender harness deliberately catching into the cavorting frills; tugging frenetically at too tight waistbands that stubbornly refused to meet; jerking at jammed zips: when has a zip ever not jammed? shuddering into icicle silk blouses; and the final trapeze act of balancing this squozen, semi-naked erection of finery on those perilous, top-heavy, crazily cramping, clicking pin heels. I could neither stand up nor lie down, and only barely sit down: drinking was not allowed, but I teetered, on my spindle legs, down the bitter blowing street, round the cruel corner, to the wild waterfront, where my previously described tavern of iniquity was. It was not normally deserted: there was not a living soul of any kind in it, neither fish, flesh nor fowl; the Padrone and his wife, as usual were eating; so I stood, all dressed up like a jaded Christmas-tree fairy, cogitating hopelessly how was I going to dispose of myself? When thankfully through the door came Joseph and his friend Ernesto, *bent* on merry-making. Ernesto was the acknowledged funny man, with a bush of sprouting hair, two enormous limpid pools for eyes, and an oversize suspending jaw; he was so much the accepted buffoon that people started to laugh the moment they saw him, though his fun was on a childishly simple level: a twisted rubber face, a spot of mock Arabic gibberish, a few clowned dialects, and an endearing personality, was enough to reduce them to helpless mirth. But he had his intensely serious side too, and when Joseph played his guitar, he would dolefully, softly, amorously, sing long impassioned songs to a would-be love rocked in the deeps of him. I was in no mood for his tame pranks, if I had drunk a barrel of brandy, I could not have smiled that night: the more

142

frolicsome he and Joseph became, the more I drew back, like an offended tortoise, into my crusty house.

How could I help remembering those other hectic, stocking-filling, children-omnipotent, senseless, Dylan always there, well out of the way of the trouble and strife, Christmas Eves; when we got drunk, quarrelled, made love, never once thinking, two fat trusting fools, of tomorrow. Now this, my tomorrow: and they wanted me to 'make gaiety'.

And even much, much further back: when I was the child, in a ferment of uncorkable excitement; not on the filling end this time, but passing interminably through that wait for the unbelievable to happen: for that limp hanging stocking to be transformed, in the dark dreaming hours, into a bulging, heavy-on-the-feet, miracle package; and the conviction that I would *never* get to sleep that night; then the inevitable disappointment next morning, that it was not exactly as my extravagant imagination had envisaged it. But our mother, who was also wonderfully extravagant, and biassed about her children, used to make us the most marvellous stockings, with always a small bottle of heavenly cherry brandy in the toe, which we drank riotously before breakfast.

Not knowing where else to go I wandered off with Joseph to the pier and the boats: my constant refuge, and I do not like to think how many times I had wearily escaped to its agitated illusion of imminent departure. And Joseph, with all his youthful intensity, his black and whiteness, his blind conviction in the importance of what he was saying, invariably started with: 'Listen, Miss Caterina,' (*senta, senti, ascolta*); and out would pour the good advice, the *consigli*, the warnings of dangerous characters, thieves, brigands, highwaymen. I did not listen to it all, but was very touched by his concern, that he should think I was worth such meticulous preservation. Nevertheless, I am afraid I was more interested in Joseph, the man, than Joseph, the narrator; and should have been infinitely more pleased, could he have stopped talking, and kissed me instead. But he was always on the look-out for spies, shady forms lurking; he said I saw nothing, when the place was bristling with them. Then a horrible doubt crossed my mind that perhaps Joseph did not want to kiss me, and this, of course, made me shrink imperceptible skins of distance away, and made my answers inexcusably curt, and even rude. Strangely, I do not think it was the case: it was rather the strict Italian division of the essentials of life: Eating, Religion, Love-making; each had its special time and place, and none must overlap into the other. On the same principle as the 'Making gaiety', you went to do a thing, and you did it; you enjoyed doing it, but under no circumstances must that thing interfere with the next thing you had to do: eating, for example; and to think there were days when I could not eat for loving!

I strongly objected, with my whole horizon a network of overlapping, to this trapdoor slamming in my face, just when I had caught one fleeting glimpse, of the sky overhead. It was an affront, a denial of nature: a kitten in a sack, with a stone in it, before its eyes were opened. Loving is so much more than the act of loving; and it was that so much more that I missed so unendurably. Then, after not getting my kiss, being subjected to a long lecture on the finer points of ethical conduct, in a hair-splitting wind: although Joseph and The Church were surface enemies, there were grisly basic resemblances between them; I was met by The Church, at my bedroom door, with snake cries of 'Prostituta, prostituta!'

Now I had missed the Beard's wife as well, come to fetch me for the midnight Mass; so, giving a last nostalgic look at Colm, sleeping so warm, peaceful, so embryonically far away, I followed my cankerous destiny. Spurned by everybody, I had a permanently guilty feeling, though I was not sure what it was about, or what I had done; whatever, it was a very fitting, self-pitying mood, in which to go and confess my sins. Clutching the floating square of fichu, which made me feel doubly conspicuous, over my head, I wrenched at the church door, which would not open, then gave, with a swing and a bang. Every head turned, it seemed, in my direction; I dared not fumble for a seat under the fire of those scorching eyes, and stood cowed at the back. I had thought it would go on for half an hour at most, but it dragged on to three quarters, then over the hour . . . when it was all too evident that the minds of the fidgeting people were filled with visions of supper and bed.

I was standing, on my jumping pins, next to the paralytic in his chair; and I was reminded of my paralytic, the one I had danced. Dancing a paralytic does sound a contradiction in bones, but the concentrated fervour compensated for that; it was in my mystic, Parisian, Isadora crank period: a throbbing combination of shrouds and sandals. I was grateful for the small mercy that Dylan had not seen me then, though he met me soon after, on my return to London, and the ridiculing word; so it died a silently punctured death. Not stone dead; for now, incorrigibly again, I saw myself, in a pure white night dress, puritanically lace-collared and slotted, lift my waxen hands, and say in mild impelling tones, to the live paralytic undeniably by my side: 'Lift up thy bed and walk'; and saw him, like myself, those ardent years ago, spasmodically twitch, by infinitesimal degrees, to Segovia's plucked strings, to his corkscrew, miraculously straightening legs; and stand there, struck with wonder and astonishment; then make the first faltering step . . . a moving testimony to my fabulous powers. It rarely failed to move me to tears, and even now I felt a wetness trickle down my cheek.

In front of me there was a sardined row of the cloistered misses of the town, pressing up against each other, like abandoned calves in a thunderstorm. They never walked in the streets alone, but always with linked arms, muffled in paint box coats, in close knit, intimately spun, plaintively lowing droves. They all wore woolly caps on the tops of their heads from which the ungovernable hair, tied, pinned, and gripped, sprang in shoots, cascades, turbulent rapids. And those unweathered faces, as though unwrapped from cotton wool, hidden in a secret drawer; which was not far from the staid reality; I marvelled again at their ability to live on this weather battered, buffeted, blasted island, as though immersed in an oriental harem.

What did they do with themselves when not on show parade, in the intermediary period, between the festa days, when they were not seen: when they gestated, and waited to be nabbed by a man; and how did they ever get nabbed, when a man was not allowed inside the house until he was engaged to one of them? These were the absorbing mysteries to me that I could never satisfactorily resolve.

This, and much more, fruitless musing passed through my head, mixed with the cracked, cheese-grater admonishing voice, of the determined to give us our money's worth priest. The press of communicants, returning from the altar rail, as though crossing a bridge in the dark with a golden cargo, that must be held preciously intact till they got to the other side. The bobbing girls, their horsetails of hair swinging, adjusting this, adjusting that, whispering buoyed-with-dew secrets, giggling, pinching, as incapable of staying still, as the stars to stop shining. And at the back the cemented wall of men, standing,

146

observing, reserving judgment. Then the rush to the holy font, the liberal dipping of fingers, the scramble of crossing; and the concerted push out the door.

It was over, and I stood shivering in the cold night again, looking in vain for the frivolous ribbons and bows of the signora Beard. She was a tiny bird woman, all feathers and nerves, perched on her tiny, aspiringly high bird heels. She had been a singer on the stage and could not forget it, when poor old Babbo: and I am sure he was older than the oldest inhabitant in the grave; then a dashing Colonello, snatched her from the 'Pomp and Circumstance' of vain display; made her his honourable wife, and gave her three strapping children; with slavery and poverty thrown in, as an afterthought. She had a valiant heart, battled to keep up appearances, in their near-stable room, for all of them; wondered wistfully, but not rebelliously, what she was missing; and craved something as simple as a little poetry in her life. Also she was more than prepared to be naughty, if given the chance, but too frightened to take the risk of being detected.

She jumped on me with her eldest boy Cesare, who was sixteen, a year older than mine, and towered above her; and they led me off, up the countless steps, to their room, for celebration supper. There I saw my first fire: three matchsticks crackling together in a minute iron basket; I huddled over the fleeting blaze, feeding it with splinters, and trying to thaw out my frozen legs. Then the festive supper began; finishing up with a ceremonial bottle of champagne, which made the round of the table, then, a thing I have never seen before, was corked up again. The music boys came with their tinkling, chestnut jokes, and Christmas smiles, setting the children in an uproar of delight; but nothing could dislodge the stone in my heart; and a more plebeian, unintoxicated night was never spent. I could not even walk back with Joseph; the Babbo insisted on clinging to my arm, and accompanying me back to the hotel door, which was barred and bolted. We banged, and banged . . . at last The Church, tousled and cross from bed, and camouflaged in wool from head to foot, opened up. I fell into bed, about four in the morning, a congealed lump of ice, and buried my groans in the roast potato warmth of Colm.

What a Christmas Day awakening! as though all the pins and needles of dissipation were pricking me, in concatenated unison. I lay there, a perforated sponge, unable to stir a muscle, moaning to myself: 'No, no, no, I shall never get up today.' And Colm bounced, and joggled me, and screamed for his bicycle: at least I had got him that, and nearly ruined myself to ease my conscience: but no stocking. They had an odd custom here of hanging the stockings up on the sixth of January, when some kind of witch creature called the Befano, was supposed to come and leave one present; the rest was padded with sweet, sick-making muck; not a patch on our treasure-filled home ones. Somehow Colm got his clothes on, without any help from me, and disappeared, with the bicycle, to the dangers of traffic, precipice, and pier: I closed my eyes to the visions of angel corpses on leafy biers; and still could not move. I knew I allowed him too much liberty, but I challenged God to try that one on me; there would be no more girding up of loins, or tightening in of belts, or pulling up of socks, then.

Then The Church came in, up since six, bluff, full of bustling cheer, as sure of his own rightness, as I of my own wrongness; he wished me a jollying '*buon Natale*'; I responded, not very encouragingly, with a flood of tears. He at once concluded I was missing the family; I was, but how much more, to be precise, one particular member of it, that I was never going to see again: did you hear *never*? What is never? To them death is death, and you don't go on about it all the time; to me, I do not know what it is. I hate it, I won't have it so.

I had the gross prospect of another vast stuffing in the Beard's room, and there was no polite way of avoiding it, apart from instant suicide, and I had not the strength for that. So by gradual circumlocuting motions, doing all the things that least needed doing first, I got myself out of the bed, and dressed into some shape.

Then above all the other bombarding noises, in the dressed-up street, I heard a peremptory voice chastising Colm for reckless riding, and that voice was shouting, 'Dylan, stop, Dylan!' and it was mine. This trick had been played on me before, and I could not stop myself; but every time it happened I had a terrible sense of his bodily proximity; just round the corner, up the road, in the next pub, about to come out, heavy-laden with bear coats, straggling mufflers, protruding papers, and boom down the street, for all the world to hear, 'Cait.'

And so to dull, plug, blunt, post haste, the too skinned-to-the-quick consciousness, with more cotton wool steps, more cotton wool food, more somnambulant wine . . . till over-replete, the torch quenched in my eyes, sick at staying on, reluctant to move to my extinguished house, I sat, as though anchored to the table. But they dragged me up the mountainside, the children, by now distraught with too much unaccustomed riches: whining, wrangling . . . the Signora struggling along behind in her unsuitable finery; the lucky Babbo nodding in his rocking chair, his feet in the cinder box; too old to bother to make an effort any more.

And startling us at this mourning-suited time of year, in a black-minded landscape: a dancing yellow mimosa tree, like a rakish wedding guest at a funeral party. And a little later I noticed, for the first time, down the

149

shelving cliffs, white blossoms, and palest pink, and at their feet, almost ashamed to show themselves at so unseemly a time, dwarf daffodils, narcissi, and cherry pie.

There is an indefinable hostility about a house that has been left, even for a day, as though it has taken offence, and is spitefully having its own back, by giving a frigid reception, in its most aloof manner; deliberately and petulantly demonstrating its ugliest flaws, its most depressing blemishes, to the guilty owner. And mine played all these capricious wiles on me, as I unwillingly forced open the door. The Beard family as always made an indecent rush to my pathetic gabinetto, which was not even blessed with a flush; but I thought sometimes it was their chief pleasure in coming, and they saved up all week for it. But this was not kind, since they had none, of any description, nor anybody else in Rio, judging by the abundance of human excrement that found its way, not only into disused buildings and abandoned sites, but into places so public I couldn't imagine how they ever got down to it! The rocks and beaches were plastered with it, so that it was impossible to find a clean space in which to sit down; even the pier was thick with it; and closer still to the town, under arches, in ditches, against walls; yes, on pavements too, and I have no doubt, that were it not for the four o'clock in the morning dustmen, with their handy ordure carts, the streets themselves would be brown Danubes.

Yet they were inveterate washers, clothes washers: don't ask me how they kept their bodies from stinking to high Gorgonzola, with those driblets of cold water; which was one of the reasons I found it necessary to go into the sea, however rebuffing, every now and then. Impossible to visualize an Italian town without the offerings and proof, from every window, of triumphant, constantly blowing, rubbed-to-the-skeleton, family wash. They did it the hard way, beating and hammering the dirt out as though it was a personal enemy, on a stone slab, with a trough of cold, hard, soap-congealing water in front of them; it was a miracle there was any garment left by the time they had let out all their spite on it. There was a public wash-house in the town, that I used to pass on my way up the zig-zag path, to the Protestant graveyard, which was sadly select and empty, onwards to my protestant solitudes. I longed to stop, and look, and ask questions; and wanted nothing better than to be one of happy unthinking them, instead of miserable thinking me; but my nerve failed me: a bunch of men is bad enough, but a bunch of women! they would surely devour me. There was a continuous coming and going of shared animation, while pounding ceaselessly at the taken for granted slave work; making me more than ever conscious of my outsider isolation. They drove me, as painfully as if they had stoned me with derision, every day further, and higher over the mountains, till I came at last to the 'Calvary'. No symbolic Calvary of the wallowing imagination, but the exact replica, I am certain, transported, stone by cypress, by cross, from Bethlehem. The long, slow, dragging upward slope, with no visible end; the faithful wall, crouched and humble, following; the stunted cypress, cone stubbled, standing severely to one side, watching; the doubled up bushes, bent kneed, prostrating themselves, the distant house from a long ago world; the ageless scattered sheep cropping the coarse tufted grass into eternity; and there must be a stray ass praying; in those haze-tranquil pastures.

But how much preferable, more noble, that heavy, rough, clean-wooded cross, knowing its burning destination; to my couple of flimsy splintering, crossed sticks, pivoting distractedly in all the directions of the syren rainbow.

The Signora too, transplanted from her fractional hub of activity, was infected with this melancholia; but she did not, like me, run to meet it, as though it was an old friend I had momentarily lost sight of; she had not learned this subtle pleasure: she simply turned her back on it, and ran; back to the town, the lights, the cheating deception of something going on.

It was getting dark now, as we stumbled unseeing down the cliff; and I remembered then, the final obligation of this taxing Christmas Day: supper in the guarded citadel of The Church family. I wanted nothing more than to put my head down, to revel in layers of blackness, to forget for a too short, closed space of time, who, and where I was; but for this supremely formal occasion I should need to summon my small stock of rectitude, the remnants of my lady's manners, and conceal myself in an armour of blotting paper, in which to sink the blunt teeth of tedium, the gaseous mouth of torpor. And when I was at my lowest ebb, mangled to a fatty wraith, yes, such a thing is possible, and no sparks flew; then the benign Church would turn on me such a disarming smile: lightning splitting up thunder was never more revealing, and say, with all the bells of heaven ringing in a joyous hymn of praise, '*Bravo, benissimo. . . .*' I only wished I could stay the way he wanted me to be. But I observed he was manfully careful never to stay long himself at these bosomy sessions: a hearty entry, a brisk look round, to make sure we were all securely chained to our posts, a quick bite, a few rallying words, and he was urgently off again . . . leaving me tugging abortively at my chain, and cursing him.

It was no good, try as I might, I could not settle down in this protected oasis; I frothed and foamed, and pawed the ground to shake it off: why I was in such a blind hurry to gallop back to my Bronte moors, crags, hollows, is one of those unanswerable questions; they plagued the soul out of me, but they were mine, and without the smell of them, I was nobody; and it is very important to be somebody; even a bad somebody. I had journeyed so far away, daily more far, from the tidily turned up, neatly hemmed in, French-seamed together, conventions; that it was too late now, to attempt the gathering together of all the frayed threads for the futile doubling back. And in my half-thrust-upon-me, half-sought segregation, there were, at incalculable intervals, rare rewards: rewards that the cushioned ones were, quite rightly, never allowed to savour; let them be content that their cushions had no pins in them. One of the lesser ones was the game of pretending to belong: joining the crowd, dressing up, dishing out the small talk, as prettily and pettily, as anybody else; taking a man . . . but this was a more risky business.

This was my weakness in the Joseph game: that instead of having to pretend that I loved him, I had to pretend, that I was pretending I did; and that is not half so easy. But the spontaneous love that had sprung up instantaneously between us, was in danger of degenerating into a farce; with the continued deriding jibes from The Church, reinforced by his strongest argument yet: 'Everybody is laughing at you.' Disapproval, that was almost too easy to take: approval would have been a lot more foreign; but laughter! I did not even mind for myself, but was Joseph strong enough to withstand that? He was strong and brave, I knew, and, for a boy of his age, his moral courage was astonishing; but I could not expect him to be as impervious as me to the rules and regulations of his upbringing, and the sacred laws of the town.

The religious meal went on; I pushed down the delicious, but surfeiting bird, which at any other time, the middle of the night, for instance, I would have devoured, bones and all: proving my contention that a chunk of dough when you want it is worth all the geese in China. Then, when I had listlessly dropped the small chat, and was sitting slumped back, trying to think of moving, they brought on the *pasta ubriaca*: drunken cake; and sticky figs, with almonds obscenely inserted into them.

The drunken cake was the best I have ever tasted, and I had seen her mixing it on the marble top of the kitchen table. She made a circling fortress of flour: the young Signora, the son's wife, who was being docilely trained in the cooking steps, of her old-timer mother-in-law; and into this round space in the middle, she poured an alarming quantity of one-third olive oil to two-thirds aleatico wine, deftly kneading in the perilous edges, as fast as they started to cave in; till a delectable soggy substance was attained; into which again was poured and folded, and buttoned up: raisins, sultanas, chopped nuts, and I don't know what other spicy rarities.

I also saw her making the ravioli: rolling out the paste flat, putting little pinched pyramids, of the green tasty filling, in regulated rows, over one half of the paste, then, with a skilful flip, flapping the other half, with perfectly judged distance, over the top; and now, squeezing in the paste round each pyramid, to fit and contain them; then, with a curling instrument, pressing down the professional notched lines in between them, down and across; and with a knife, easing out the now gently separated, miraculously liberated, shop-dapper ravioli squares. If only, I thought, I could do something as well as that, just one thing, I would go on doing it without stopping. But I could just imagine my ham-handed efforts, sweeping everything off the table as though a tank had passed through: the clever ones did all their subtle economical movements, on a small cleared corner, with a haphazard assurance, and an annoyingly casual certitude; stacking up my tools and materials in mountainous formation, as though preparing a battlefield, which indeed I was; I was a despot for strict order and organization. Then pummelling, stirring, beating, with Carnera brutality; till the bit of limp, greying, winded paste I was working on so furiously had not a hope in my kitchen furnace of rising: it lay stiff, defeated, leaden-eyed, like a run-over rat, at the bottom of the sweating bowl.

If I tried any of the other suitable arts intended by nature, I am told, for women, it was just as bad: sewing, for instance; I deliberately assumed that very necessary inconsequential, thoughts-elsewhere, expression, briskly threaded my needle; or did I not? Not me, in spite of all my dodges, it would not go in; then, when it did, out of sheer capriciousness; and I made the first meticulous stitch, which could not possibly go wrong, it inconceivably stuck; the cotton performed a frenzied trapeze act: it knotted itself up for a start; then performed a ballet of lighthearted twirls and pirouettes, maypole entangling the lost knot; and always a stray loop managed to hook itself on some fantastically far off, sticking-out point; put there on purpose to send my head reeling and spinning dizzily, into rages of space.

And the clothes I bought, which imperatively had to be wool, the hardest and dearest thing to get: coming from the home of wool, pumped up with pretty cotton illusions about this island; they, without having the civility to wait to be put on, burst at the seams, the buttons flew off, the hems sagged down, and they shrank to wooden straitjackets under the vigorous stone

155

washings. I was in danger of becoming a British Diehard, like the Englishman, and preaching on the virtues of durability. The most gratifying garments that I had succumbed to eventually, against all my feminine coynesses, were the pink woollen all-embracing underwear; which in my deluded days, I should not have been seen dead in, but which now, in my nobody-caring-enough-to-impress days, I would not have been seen alive without. And, without exaggeration, never that, I don't think I could have survived without them. When I think of my daily wind-splitting climbs up the put-to-try-me steps, to my hibernating-till-the-summer house; my sitting hunched over my broken pot of coaxed and blown to life small coal; the over expansive, bland sea gazing scathingly at me; and me gazing in despair at my chapped and swollen hands, the poison bursting from behind the rotting nails. Colm and I had both been infected with this Jobian bug, whose quaint fancy it was to choose us, of all suffering people; with five hours to kill in front of me. Time was so slow that sometimes I thought it had stopped for bad and all; a sheet of spiteful paper prancing in the wind; and a bottle of black, as they call red here, wine gulped down; with chunks of crusty bread, absorbing cheese, and crackling greenery; to keep the cold satisfied, and to envelop the petrified mind in an icy film of muzziness. I thought how incongruous that I, perched, like an Edith Sitwell heron, on one leg, on the edge of nowhere, should be accused by The Church of loose and profligate tastes; while, out of the length and breadth of the town, he could not have picked a more unloved, and, whether by virtue of necessity or not, scouredly chaste creature.

I thought irrelevantly about the sunny letters from England, hoping I was more settled, coming to terms with life: what does that mean? Finding a modicum of happiness; what *is* that? A Valentino? all against a background of dates and palms, and languorous tangoes. I was glad they could not see me now; and how would I dare go back, as raw, as sore, as unsewn up, as I had ever been, if not more.

How was I going to weather the next three cutting in two months: January, February, March; the land would just be waking up, stretching out of its frowning coma, as I was due to leave for my weeping land of Wales. And I felt that, however hard and cruel this was, or the next place I might plant my scaly body in, I never, never wanted to go back there; I had as much Dylan as I could carry with me.

XIV

THE money was going at an alarming pace as usual; and, unless I did some illegal wangling, I could not hold out. I did such idiotic things: went across the water, a mad adventure, and my first venture out of the island, to the Continent. Solely to find a reputable chemist, in which to buy face creams and powder, and other essential disguises and fripperies; and naturally I ignored my list, and bought a heap of unnecessary luxuries as well. A reaction against my thorn-strewn wilderness; including a five-thousand-lire bottle of 'Scandal', which did me quite that sum of moral good, as I poured it profusely down my clinging, pink woollen vest. A thing is worth, I decided, exactly how much you want it. Then: the buying lust was on me now, and I could not get rid of the dirty stuff fast enough; I bought a pretty, but quite useless, bathing costume, a pair of butterfly winged brassieres, which could not possibly last more than a day, and the purest, sheerest silk stockings, to tear and rip on my shaggy mountains. So I managed to whittle away a tidy not-to-be-sneezed-at sum; what with fares of bus, boat, and carozza, and the sustenance of the wilting spirit; which, in my island fortress, would have lasted me a good stretch longer. It was a queer, uncanny feeling, being free on the Continent, making me self-consciously aware of my banished island stripes; and, like a disorientated prisoner, I fled back, almost with relief, a perverted sense of homecoming, to my cell.

What a warming pleasure to see Joseph waiting for me: it made me feel for a moment that he belonged to me, and I wanted to run up to him, put my arms round him, and the two of us go off together. Instead of which we gave each other a stilted 'Good evening', and I went off into the bar, to drink with indifferent people. The person I loved most I had to keep furthest away from: why is that an almost infallible rule?

Then there were the dolls; and nobody could say I was suffering from a thwarted maternal complex; but they were so beautiful, I simply could not resist them. I had already bought six, and they were by no means cheap, anything from three thousand lire up. I had sent the best ones to my Aeron daughter, more beautiful and wicked than any of the dolls; and the rest distributed in the town, to various seductive little girls, including Joseph's two youngest sisters. He was the only boy among four sisters; and I had a sudden terrible thought: would they think I was trying to buy Joseph? But if ever a boy was painfully honest: even his lies were honest; puritanical and unbudgeable, it was Joseph. I kept for myself only a small mulatto beauty, with flowers in her hair, and gold ear-rings, who said 'Mama' with human conviction. And I kidded myself she would bring me luck; but my doll fetish hardly came under the heading of essentials, like the wool. It was as though half of me wanted to get rid of all I had, as fast as possible, so that I should be forced back to England; and the other half was rooted fast, and stubbornly refused to budge, fancying that the accumulation of hardships must achieve something, though I should have been hard put to say what, except an even more disgruntled character.

In the midst of these spending orgies the Englishman, whom I had put right out of my mind, and thought never to see again, came back for the New Year.

We met like long lost, verging on incestuous, brother and sister; he was so absurdly English-seeming after his short sojourn there, even more contrastingly so. I wondered if I stood out as determinedly freakish from my background as he did; and, though I ardently wished to be as vampish and slinky as their women, I was afraid I did.

I searched keenly for signs of disappointment in him with the 'Old Country'; but he jocularly sported a Harris tweed fisherman's hat, swore by the Scotch whisky, in spite of its prohibitive price, and insisted that England had the best food in the world, and he'd had a decent meal at last, remarking, in evidence, that he felt 'as fit as a flea'.

He had come back loaded with pathetic, and truly touching mementoes of Britain: tins of Bird's custard, which the Italians lapped up, believing it a rare delicacy: packets of staff-of-the-earth porridge; I can't think what they made of that, unless they floated it on the top of their hot water 'brodo' soup; Worcester sauce, and all the fire-eating ingredients for a pukka curry. He invited us, minus children, canny as ever, with the other magnates of Rio: doctor, post office, and big business; to come to his house for dinner, and sample his self-made 'Indian', anti-Ity, curry.

As long as he was amiable, his blue eyes twinkling in his ruddy face, he was a tolerably lovable monster; but if it ever became a matter of serious conviction, we took opposite sides; and had there been a war, we would straightaway have bayoneted each other. I still found offensive, and impossible to swallow, in spite of its pitiable aspect, his intolerable statement that he would not have louts, meaning Joseph, sitting at his table, nor any member of the working class. I still preferred them to any other classes, in spite of the knocks I had had from their dumb fists. Surely it was more praiseworthy to be working than not? than standing, an idle desiccated gentleman, on an abortive pier all day, waiting for fish that never came, because, as he well knew, they were poisoned in the contaminated water.

But the trouble was, however much we basically disagreed, and would have disowned each other in England; on this foreign raft we were bound unwillingly together, by the rough cords of the lost, the disowned, the white untouchables. And there passed between us the terrible recognition, veiled in shrieking pleasantries, that one drowning man casts on his drowning comrade.

This wet exchange brings back to me the similarly powerful suffocations of that drowning Sunday. The rain belted down all night, like an enraged mother; and I thought, when morning came, it can't possibly keep it up; as soon as it clears I will go for a long salutary walk in the mountains, before the dissipations of Sunday begin. The week-end always caused a slackening in our would-be rigid rules: the combination of Dickens school for Colm, and vestal virgin banishment for me in the campagna. I felt that if things were tough enough for me, it was not so bad deserting him to his babble of tongues, for a child's eternity; but if I had been enjoying myself, I should have felt terrible about him, not that he would have been any better or worse off; and if there was, by any chance, an out-of-season streak of wrongly balming sun for me to drowsily forget time and myself in, for the briefest spell; then I was struck with remorse at the injustice I had done him.

But the rain did not stop; it went on, against all the laws of logic, and the findings of physical phenomena. On, and on, and On: where was it coming from? and what was I going to do? There were really only two alternatives: one, to go back to bed, of which I was defeatedly in favour, but could not with Colm; the other, to go out in it, and get drowned, which I would have preferred, but dared not drag the children to their deaths with me. There were other children too, don't worry; till two o'clock in the afternoon my wilting dissolute, giving up its cold-blooded ghost, hotel bedroom, was honoured with the presences of the three strapping Beard children. They were roughly the same ages as mine, but that was no excuse to saddle me with them; if I had to have such ill-assorted sprouts of nature I would rather have had my own: I had a morbid interest in them. They had come, they said, since ten in the morning, to collect me for the institution Sunday Beard lunch, in case, as they rightly surmised, I might be tempted to escape. There was always a birthday, or a *festa*, or some unswervable excuse for it; and I always got the faintly nauseating feeling that they had served up that extra repulsive she-hound, with the flapping dugs, in, I almost fancied, the recognizably tasty dish. As I stepped out of their dripping shack into the gushing wind, it occurred to me that the one thing that was essential in this island was an umbrella: at the first spot of rain a gaudy forest of them popped up, of all shapes and sizes and colours. But I did not care how bedraggled I got: I refused to succumb to the final signposts of respectability: goloshes and umbrellas; my woollen vests went dowdily far enough.

When I had parked Colm and Chico, the youngest Beard, in the cinema, I turned my face, and bare head, resolutely into the driving blizzard; and trudged blindly up the flowing mountainside. I was aiming instinctively for the Calvary, as the only place worthy to match the tempests of the day; when at a bend in the climbing, twisting, duskily blotted out path, I met Joseph. I thought how brave of him to come out in all this rain, just to meet me, because the Italians are like cats in the wet: their fur shudders, at a drop of water, as though they were being stroked the wrong way; unlike the wallowing and revelling of the vulgar British dogs. For me it would have been much braver to face the rain of dissecting eyes drenching me, from the Sunday cloud of fork-tongued townspeople.

So we went on together, Joseph and me, for once not feeling watched, in our private rain world, with spies crouching in every thicket. We thrust into deeper, sheltering woods, lay on the soaking earth and clotted leaves, fought against enveloping crackling clothes, for one brief meeting of the flesh: one taste of wordless warmth to last us another week. The wetness, and our fumbling urgent caresses were so mixed up that I speculated, whilst gazing intently up into a dripping bush: how unreasonably the promptings of nature depended on artificial assistance; and I thought how wonderful to be in a warm bed with Joseph, with only a nightgown on. Then the hurried gathering together of the dispersed self, the pretending it had never happened, harum-scarum remarks, and the jubilant dash into the dark; stopping for the first friendly kiss, and on, stumbling, excitedly suddenly, down the Calvary. The parting of the ways, for him to sidle back into the town one way, me another; then to meet on the street later with cool astonishment, greater strangers to each other than any odd body passing by.

I was still not sure why there was the necessity for this elaborate subterfuge: who was I accountable to? I had nobody to deceive, except The Church, and I did not legally belong to him. But he tied me up in unwritten laws, twice as unbreakable; with his lewd, tongue-wagging, screaming with derisive laughter images; that he dangled, flaunted, lacerated me with, seeking to put me to eternal shame; and very nearly succeeding. Till I considered, was it so bad for a woman to want, to need a little loving, since that is the purpose, I am always being told, she is destined for? If she goes to the opposite extreme, and concentrates on a career, that is even less popular; so all that is left is the veil, which puts her out of circulation altogether; or the equally exempt from society, but incomparably more loveless, brothel. I knew exactly what I should do to please all the mothers-in-law on earth: shut myself in a box for the rest of my life and never be seen again; in which 'sacred' seclusion murder could be committed with impunity, as long as it was not *seen*. The murder itself mattered not a fig, but the sight of it did; gave offence to that nebulous 'They' that hovered untraceably and omnipotently in the void. But I could not forget I had only one life to live: torn to bits as it was: though apparently everybody else could.

Then, in a wanton delirium for Rio, I joined the steadies permanently sitting in the Café window, for all to see, and to see all, bovinely stomaching the coffee from an hour ago. As always, the regular entrenchment of the Beard family were there, and once again I pondered, How did they do it, or rather, how had they done it? conceived these solid amazon children. The Englishman bluff and hearty, doing his heavyweight British act; but I had to admit he was the only one who drank, and carried on a semblance of a conversation while the Italians stared hypnotized at us. Was it better after all to do a conscious damage: rubbing wits, exchanging the mermaid's soap of pooled knowledge; or relaxing on harmonious digestive organs, with pouting lips, and serene doe eyes, saying nothing?

There was Pietro-Petruchka for instance, as adorable as the angel of the Annunciation, with a smile emblazoning heaven, contemplating, in his guily-wiley mind, which never missed an opportunity to cultivate the most profitable person, exactly what he was going to eat for supper; and he twirled his rolled umbrella: for already middle-aged habits nibbled at him; as though it was a wand.

And Alfeo, who looked the nearest thing to an old-fashioned artist in Rio; with his shock of hair, lithe emaciated body, and tapering eagle-nailed fingers, which must surely rhapsodize the guts out of some string instrument; but no, he was connected with the mines too, though not actually hacking in the tunnels. He was the one, I had been warned, might go off his head at any moment: hence the immediate sympathy between us; and he was periodically taken away to be locked up. With children he was a wizard: with no noise, or coercion, they were spellbound by him, as, paying no attention to them whatsoever, and murmuring gently to himself, he built the most fantastic fairy-tale palazzos out of Colm's bricks.

And Anna Maria, the daughter of the proprietors of the café: elephantinely fat Francesco, who belied the myth of fat people being jolly and endearing, by consistently swindling me over my change: and his mealy-mouthed wife. She emerged from this debauch of the flesh pots as a superbly voluptuous Venus, whose rearing breasts strained mountainously against her clinging jumpers; and I felt sure one day they would triumph; whose slope of richly promising hips swung invitingly to and fro, like a lovesick pendulum; and nobody, man or woman, could see her without thinking how delicious she was. Only the type of women who put newspapers over the best carpet would be capable of damping down her seam-splitting beauty; as for the men, they one and all ocularly undressed her, put her to bed, and glutinously masticated her: she was the larger than life embodiment of their sweaty dawn cravings. I tried to imagine who would eventually be the envied possessor of this magnificent creature; but, what seems often to be the punishment in these bountifully blessed cases, she was claimed by a tuppenny-halfpenny squirt from the mainland, with a flashy tie and a motor car; and the beautiful long-legged, raven-locked, red-dust-booted miners yearned in vain.

It was everybody's birthday at once: first, the Signora Beard, and I bought a bottle of champagne for her, then the Englishman quickly remembered he'd had one yesterday, and I bought a bottle of champagne for him; then Alfeo said it was his tomorrow, and I bought a bottle of champagne for him; they lapped it up obediently after the preliminary moans of disgust, and consecutive clucking noises to indicate how contrary it was to all their better feelings: indispensable to Italians if they ever do you the honour of accepting a drink. There was not the remotest hope in Rio Inferno of anybody returning the offer, and for this kind of impulsive gesture, which had no forethought or afterthought to it, I earned my reputation for loose profligacy and libertinism from the very ones, most likely, who were profiting from it. I did not care, why should I? My not caring was my strength, and they could not understand that I did not care about the things which were life and death to them: I had had my death, and any dying after that was an afternoon nap.

However, they did show tiny twinklings of being starrily lit up, not that the talk became any more brilliant; the Signora began to gabble very loud, the Englishman went redder and pushed his fishing hat to the back of his head, Petruchka's heaven-sent smile crystallized on his face, and Alfeo's hands clawed and clutched at his old newspapers of a long-ago air-liner disaster. For him it was not disastrous, but something miraculous, and he pored over his cuttings and pictures with reverent love: the three young groomed women wrapped in sheets, heads hanging backwards, hair rippling down over the mortuary slabs; I began to see, with his eyes, there was a strange terrifying beauty in it. But there is that about kinked people, a muffled tediousness, as though they were talking to you, from under a pile of eiderdowns, at the bottom of the bed, that makes it hard to concentrate on what they are saying, and primitively repels.

As for me, it was one of my cushion days, everything sank in only too easily, but nothing came out; and between the lot of us it was little enough we were getting. I quietly mused, how lovely to have a bottle of champagne all to myself one day, preferably on getting up in the morning! And I remembered, in spite of myself, how Dylan and I had lain in bed imagining, especially when we were terribly broke, how wonderful it would be if we could lie there all day, with an immaculate waiter bringing us champagne first thing in the morning ... a continuous cinema on the ceiling, appetizing titbits, interspersed with love, and buckets of drink, till night fell on our bemused wickedness. But it never came to pass, we were always too poor, and we always had too many children. I felt I had never loved him so closely, and I wanted to undo all the wrongs I had done him, and sew on all the buttons, darn all the socks, listen to all his complaints, with gratitude. If distance lends enchantment, rubs out the cross purposes of two waning personalities, then how was it that he had never been less distant?

And the rain went on, out of sheer cussedness, and the oranges shook, and wept, melancholy out of place, as though suddenly Wales had had a daft inspiration to transform herself into the Italian riviera overnight.

Another week began. And with it the trudging and trying to begin all over again the interminable new life: faultless, abstemious, harmonious; which always somehow ended up as the old life. It was not so much that this state of trance-like being was so impossible to attain, and when attained was too restful to be true; but that it left so much insufferably wide-awake time: and that had got to be dodged, dimmed, dully anaesthetized for me. There was a limit to confronting face-to-face the monotonous lumber cluttering up my head, under grey, hulking dust sheets.

The tunnels that bored through the mountains round Rio had much in common with the musty burrowings in my brain. I had at last summoned up the courage to ask permission on my own to visit one; it was for me a big effort, as I had an instinctive aversion to going underground, and Italian officialdom is worse than all the others rolled into one. To buy a postage stamp creates a major crisis; as for sending a doll to England, I thought I should never finish filling up the identical form, nine hundred and ninety nine times: what can they do with them all? So to get my permit for the tunnels, the preliminary inevitability was: 'Wait a moment,' indicating a bench, where several 'contentissimi' Italians had been waiting for the past four or five hours, only too grateful for a sit down. I saw this was a case for speech, rapid and vehement, if senseless: the problem was to find a victim to launch the speech at. In the meantime I was scrabbling in my basket for some occupational therapy, not being blessed with the Divine Content of the Italians. A harassed man, waving papers, hurried from the office on urgent business; without giving him a chance to escape, I planted myself in front of him, and started in on him, emphasizing the one important name at my disposal. That, and the obvious nuisance I was making of myself, were the only things he understood; and I cannot blame him, as my very limited store of Italian, when I was worked up, overflowed into some unheard-of garbled language. But the fanatical undertone eventually had some effect: I had made up my mind by then I was bound to get into the tunnels; first they said Yes, they would give me the permit, but would I sit down and 'wait a moment'. I was not going to be fobbed off so easily, or I should never have got to the country that day, and would be sitting there still. So I said, with great impatience, that I could not possibly wait, with all the pressing important work I had to do: as I thought shamefacedly of my bits of flimsy fluttering paper in the wind; but it was essential to keep up the bluff that I was engaged on some highly significant job. So they agreed then to send the permit to the hotel for me later.

However, when I got back that evening, the cowards had sent an underling to say they were sorry, but women were not allowed in the tunnels: they were too dangerous, the tunnels. And now I was really annoyed, and determined to get the better of them, as a point of honour. So the next morning there I was again, and this time I insisted on seeing the Director. They prevaricated for some time about his whereabouts, inventing vaguely and volubly to avoid giving me a straight answer; and to guard his sacred invisibility from crude exposure to me; till I began to wonder did he, in fact, exist. But I had a very strong impression he was sitting behind the office door at the back, owlishly listening to every word of our discussions. Still I stood there, and would not go. In the end, seeing they could not get rid of me, in spite of all their sly dissuasions and calculated descriptions of the dangers, to which I replied loftily: 'So the lives of the men who go to work there every day do not matter? I am not so vain I think mine matters more.' At least I tried to say that, and they either did not understand, or pretended not to; but they capitulated. I had no fear for myself: I knew I could trip across the Niagara Falls, blindfold, and drunk, with impunity: God is not interested in taking the lives that have ceased to matter, and mine would not have been a very enviable tassel in His nightcap.

Nevertheless, I diverted myself with my favourite fancies: giant rocks almost submerging me, almost mind, I had to know what was going on, while frantic gangs dug me out, led by Joseph. The limp Ophelia drooping: in death I entirely forgot my boots and clenched fists; carried blanched, hair entangled with minerals, dropping iron gems, on my 'dark' passage to the ambulance. And, best of all, the deathbed scene: the shaded, bluish light, the hushed conspiratorial voices, the blinking, millions of miles away window, the bulging sea-sick walls, the starched-front uniforms, the low muttering of delirium, and the dry cough. In the next scene I painlessly merged from Ophelia into Greta Garbo in *Camille*. And now there was no holding me: I was not only mangled and maimed, though the symmetry of figure and feature remained intact, I had also mysteriously developed the romantic symptoms of consumption; cutting out the blood spitting. In a revealing, swansdowny, billowing négligé, I gasped for breath, moaned, called hoarsely, huskily, broken with sobs, for an extraordinary individual, who was a cross between Marlon Brando and a college Professor. It is not only men who never grow up.

But all this talk of danger in the tunnels had given to Joseph's life a tragic poignancy; and to my love for him, which was in no need of encouragement, a new unbearably moving quality.

They told me to come back tomorrow at four, and the Director himself would conduct me, with Alfeo in tow.

This was most disappointing news for me, as I had set my heart on going to Joseph's tunnel, much further away, and seeing him working on the morning shift: they worked in eight-hour shifts: from eight in the morning till four; and from two in the afternoon till ten; but I dared not make any more fuss, and, after signing a paper to say I went at my own peril, I said I would be there.

After school the next day, with Alfeo and Colm, who refused to be dumped, I went to the office again, and some type of smarmy sub-official took charge of us. The Director, if indeed there was one, remained anonymous throughout. We climbed the steps, and the red-dusty, winding road up the nearest mountain; till we came to a kind of platform, where lorries trundled up and down, discharging their loads, to be washed and separated: the residue gushing in liquid chutes, to spread an angry rash in the sea. The sub-official commandeered one of the lorries to drive us to the top, to the opening of the tunnel: zig-zagging up a narrow break-neck precipice, to the immeasurable delight of Colm, who kept crying out: 'faster, faster, faster. . . .'

I was very grateful afterwards I had left him in the lorry, and not taken him in the tunnel. We changed into old coats, collected lamps, and set off down the small, loosely long-ago bolstered-up opening into the cemetery of the earth; getting steadily more obscure and airless as we advanced. I stepped very gingerly on the squelching mud, and if I had let myself, could have got very near to panic. I felt the spirit being sucked out of me by the descent from daylight, but there was no turning back now. The makeshift roof pressed down lower, on top of us, till even I could not stand upright: and the soaking walls, dripping with mould, closed in on us. I was not enjoying it one bit, and could scarcely breathe in the suffocating iron-sodden atmosphere; I kept wondering

171

where the men working could possibly be. At last we came on two boys loading rocks into a truck: they were helmeted, against the frequent caving in of the tunnel, which was stinking with rot, decay, and negligence. A criminal subterranean relic of supposedly extinct slave conditions. What could the lifers' prison be like in this barbarous country? It could not, by any stretch of imagination, be worse. They were pathetically young, these queer dehydrated creatures from a geological underworld: the same, and yet not the same, when they emerged above ground. I began to realize what a strong pull this warren of mountains had over the superficial bubbling overflow of the outside town; what a potent, powerful influence it was, shadowing the lives of the people.

'But where,' I asked, 'are the rest of the men?' I kept expecting sweating, semi-naked, crouched torsos, hammering at the bottom of the next long, empty, abjectly depressing tunnel. It was perhaps the emptiness that was the most heartbreaking aspect; but even worse to credit that living human beings had ever been there, or might conceivably come again. I was told that they were economizing on the late shift, and could only afford a handful of men, which made the deplorable conditions more dismal still, if that was possible. Suffering in numbers is not nearly so agonizing, as suffering singly. All the same, I had been cheated out of the thing in action, which I had come to see; and ruins are of no interest to me. So when we got back, unbelievably, to the keenly piercing night air, and chill was never so welcome, I protested that I must go in the morning, to see the men working; and, my wily mind racing, I stipulated that I should like to visit one that I had heard was a very fine tunnel: it was Joseph's of course. His pallor, dreamy green ringed eyes, and premature

172

maturity, sitting uneasily on his boyish, not over-growing yet, unset bones, was ghastly clear to me now. After twenty minutes in the tunnel I came out as parched as a corpse from a month's entombment; so what about Joseph, who spent eight hours out of every day, except Sundays, in his tomb; with the prospect of doing so for the rest of his cramped, constricted and curtailed life. That the majority of men did not consciously suffer, or complain, except at the lowness of the wages, did not think that an unpardonable wrong had been done to them, hardly thought at all, beyond the immediate doing of what had to be done, to provide the insufficient money to eat, did not detract from, or make any less, the outrage of that wrong. But Joseph did rebel, he hated it, and wanted to get out, above everything. The thought of him mouldering on there, a stooped Lycidas, through the years, was unthinkable. He clung to me, I sadly suspected, as the solitary link with the outer, wider world.

Whether his attachment, I have not the courage to call it love, to me was dependent on my stepping-stone value or not; he was set on mastering English for his future escape. How is it possible to be young, in the best sense, without being selfish, and egoistical? While the youth grows less, the egoism lingers on, and disagreeably grows more. I wanted to help him, all I could, primarily to get out of that stifling tunnel; and secondly to loose him on the seductions of civilization, knowing that this would mean the death of him to me, and me to him. As the death was coming anyhow, and it is very important to give a person the thing they think they want, I pre-ferred to speed it up, achieving some imagined good, and get it over with.

It was all very well to have these noble intentions, with which I was heavily peppered; but when I came to reflect afterwards on my sky-scraping statements: that I was most certainly going to America next year; that I had devoutly finished with England for evermore; and that I had a lot of rich friends over there: who, for instance? Who would be only too delighted to put him up, and look after him when he got there; they were based on a wilfully closed cobweb-woven future. He was very ambitious, quick-witted, and enthusiastic, with grand ideas for getting out of this one-eyed hole of Rio, with its restricting limitations; and getting into a wider, richer, more promising world. Who can blame him? He would undoubtedly need help on his arrival, and I should have loved to have been able to help him, but my own position, of which he had no conception, being what it was: it was I who needed help incomparably more than him.

My predicament was accentuated by my chronic fear of friendship, even when offered spontaneously from the heart, with no Dylan tags attached. But I had developed a deep-rooted suspicion that Dylan was at the back of and coloured all such pleasant demonstrations, and of course, to a large extent it was true; and, like all prodigiously vain people, packed with false pride, I wanted to be loved for myself alone. So, not only did I intensively not cultivate people, I went out of my way to offend them; and if they seemed, to my perverse mentality, of too privileged a posh loaded class, to insult them; then I was surprised and hurt that they did not like me, and called me aggressive. Thus, largely by my own efforts, and keeping myself at a Tibetan distance, I had achieved almost complete friendlessness. Very childish and stupid, considering I needed friends above everything.

At least in the island I could not say I was befriended because of Dylan: I saw no subversive signs of intellectual

174

activity whatsoever, not one positive book, no printed matter beyond a newspaper; I began to think it was only the Englishman and me, who not only drank, but read as well, though our literature was mostly magazines. Not a soul knew, or was interested to know, about Dylan's writing: they knew only about his death in the newspapers, and that was the end of that.

If Joseph ever did get civilized, and sophisticated, God forbid: I had a terrible vision of him, in his stripy, shiny clothes making wise-cracks; he would lose every tug of his overpowering tunnel charm, and I should not want him any more. He might even, and this was a yet more sadistic vision, by losing his native pride and aristocracy, gaining a cheap top layer of potted plausibility, achieve, in the process, that common word: commonness. And with it that self-belittling phrase: 'I was ashamed to be seen in his, or her, company.' Not, please, that I have ever said, or would, may I drop down dead, ever say it; but once a person becomes socially embarrassing, it is very hard to preserve their glamour. I remembered the Irish, and what happened to them, when they made their impulsive rush from the bogs of Ireland to the streets paved with gold of America: from peasant to glorified peasant, but always pre-eminently peasant. To cut off the corners, chisel down, mould, clip, trim, pinch the accent, purse-precious, neutralize, polish uniform the Irish, is an uphill job, and they invariably betray themselves. They are wedding-ringed to the broguey cooing of their own voices.

Whatever disastrous transformation Joseph suffered, I knew he should not be prevented going: it is very important to foster the urge for movement, change, adventure; and though I might think his new status was a tragedy, he might be very happy with it himself, be deluded he was really getting somewhere: besides it was his destiny to play with, not mine, and he would have to work it out himself. The crime of his tunnel was far more pernicious and life-damaging, than the crime of vulgarity.

XV

JOSEPH'S first small betrayal of me came after the dance: believe it or not, an honest to God dance in the strictures of Rio. First he did all he could to persuade me not to go, and I began to smell a tiny wriggling worm of suspicion. If he'd had an inkling of my character he would have known he was irrevocably challenging me to go; there was no getting out of it now, though I had been doubtful about it before. His reasons were not clearly defined but I suspected a combination of fear at accompanying me, being visibly compromised in front of the correct bunches of families and friends: though he emphasized, a little too forcibly perhaps, that it was only my interests he was concerned about; and, nearer the craven marrow, I am sure, that I would drink too much, and do something awful and scandalous.

So I deliberately ignored his hypocritical prating and went ahead with plans to go with my buddy, the Signora Beard; although we had nothing under the sun, moon, stars, or constellations, to talk about, and Alfeo. I was still half in dread of the probable chasms of embarrassment in store for me, but there was no turning back now.

The first setback came when I went to try on one of my dresses, and there was not the remotest hope of doing it up. Had I literally swelled so much? Surely it must have shrunk! But when I tried on some others, not one would meet: I had to call the Signora to the bedroom,

LL—M

and together we pulled and tugged, and ripped at zips, and split sides, and let in bits, till at last I was trussed taut like an overstuffed, autumn chicken about to crack the drawn skin asunder.

However, it was not as bad as I had expected, with my cheerful pessimism; in spite of being burdened with her eldest son, Cesare: seesawing brashly between infantile pranks, and manly precocity. To start with we had a table, and that was a haven, up among the chosen and the lost: all eyes and no partners. But the satisfaction of belonging to this privileged group does not compensate for the enormity that the rabble are dancing merrily below, and you are not. For what a woman desperately wants at a dance, though she may desperately deny it, is to dance: and I don't mean flirt, or snatch a man off somebody else; that is secondary and incidental. As long as the partner she is dancing with is not grotesquely ludicrous, and can keep in time, she is content. If, by some miraculous fluke, she gets a man who is presentable, and dances naturally, without her having to anticipate his every caper; she wants nothing better than to go on dancing with him for ever and ever after.

I hoped that being in this select, mostly married: which was as good as saying dead and gone; and many attractive, group of women, who covertly turned their backs on me; would not prejudice my participation in the enviably spinning and jiggling lower strata. They sat at their barren tables, uncontaminated by the stain of a glass, discursing brightly, with a quarter of their avid, missing nothing, attention. I ordered some of the comparatively cheap, and quite effective, Spumante, and gradually began to feel that it didn't matter so much if anybody took any notice of me or not. These downtrodden women were at heart, I began to feel, all sweet and charming, more to be pitied than condemned; but when, from the excess of my flowing generosity, I turned to one and asked her to share a drop, she stared panic-stricken at the others for collaboration, and precipitately produced the old stomach and liver excuses: did they think I had not got either? Then Cesare started getting above himself again and chucking *coriandoli*, confetti, into our mouths, and glasses; and a kind anonymous man asked me to dance.

Once on the floor my troubles were over, I might even begin, surprisingly, to enjoy myself. The perfect partner did amazingly come along: tall, dancing with no effort, and just the right proximity. But it stopped all too soon, and I had to suffer Mister's out-of-the-ark charlestoning, Alfeo's trembling skeleton, and Mario's fat sweaty body bouncing against me: but I did not mind him, and who was I to talk of bouncing fat? Fat squat people nearly always dance a lot better than long thin ones: they are paradoxically lighter, more plastic, with a pliant rhythm. But my tall perfect partner was a glorious exception: and we were performing a treat together on the 'at a distance' system, making up our own steps independently, and joining together every now and then for a twirl, which is a lot more fun. I had got to the dawn of the beautiful not caring, but fully aware, stage, which degenerates so imperceptibly into the doing something unpermissible stage. I forgot, for a second, that I was in Italy doing my incomprehensible penance, that death hung, like a tightening noose, about my neck: I was wickedly, briefly, and artificially happy.

I did nothing terrible, but for this momentary spurt of high spirits, I was severely reprimanded afterwards by the policeman, who had his orders to watch me closely. 'I am speaking,' he said unctuously, 'to you as a sister.' Joseph, torn between terror and irresistible desire not to be out of it, had abandoned his excuse of a sick nephew, three weeks old incidentally; and was trying, with 'ton of bricks' subtlety, to lure me outside, with promises of more Spumante, which I knew, even then, were lies. The passion for dancing was in me, I got stubborn, and refused to go; besides, I was cross with him for his cowardly behaviour. But there were plenty of juicy dolled-up repercussions the next day. It was reported to me by the Colonel later that Joseph had said my antics were scandalous, or words to that effect. From anybody else such a remark would not have perturbed me unduly, but for him to turn traitor on me was unforgivable. I worked myself into a selfrighteous fury, decided this was the chance I had been waiting for to put an end to us. Never while others abused him, but when he abused me; well, I had no honourable choice. But, biggest incentive of all, I must have my revenge.

As a start, I broke my usual date with him at the pier, when I came back from the country, and he came out washed and worse, from his house after work; and I failed to turn up at Gigi's: the hole in the wall by the water, our next meeting place. So I did not see him till after dinner in the café, when he came up sheepish, sweet, and commiserating. I gave him no chance to wheedle the old Italian snake charm on me, and set to without a pause; with no idea in my head what I was going to say, or in what language; but the essence of a good speech is not sense, but the conviction behind it, and the flow of words; hesitation is fatal; also the volume is important. Mine had all these, in a mixture of Italian and English, and the effect was gratifying: the people all stopped talking to listen, not that this was exceptional; but I knew it was the one thing that would upset Joseph most; much more than my words, and he kept muttering miserably, 'Not now, please, come outside, I will explain.' But he was not getting off so easily, I had my say, with the insistence of a record stuck in a groove, turned grandiosely, wished everybody a polite good night, and frog-ballooned out.

As soon as I got to my room the bombast left me, I saw his peaked, and piqued, face; said to myself, with cynical bravado: 'That's done it,' and the pain invaded me. Then I thought of Joseph in the pitiless hours of the morning, begrimed underground, worrying in his tunnel, about me; and my cocky little triumph drooped crestfallen. There are frequent times I could take a chopper and chop myself unconscious, for that demon in me that makes me deliberately do spiteful, disruptive and primarily silly actions, that hurt nobody so much as myself. I waited that night, fearful of what he would do next; so long as he did not go dead and aloof on me, I did not mind: his estranged indifference was the most intolerable; any abuse was better than that.

So now, I sat at my table outside, in the deepening welcome of dusk, trying to survive the cold a little longer, with gloves, and stove, and blaring music, till I should have to close the door on myself, and my inescapable manias. I heard a nervous voice calling: 'Catalina, Catalina'; it was Joseph, he came round the house like an amateur actor, over-acting a dramatic rôle, flapping a bloodstained finger in front of me. 'What is the matter?' I said, with, I hoped, contrastingly calm sang-froid; divining my capitulation was inevitable, I did not want to show him too soon signs of slackening in my firm resolve to cast him out.

'Come to the Calvary,' he said imperatively, 'I will explain everything.' But I would not move.

'If you have anything to say to me,' I said, 'you can say it here.'

The poor boy wriggled and squirmed, his distress was a moving picture to watch: he told me he had been to the

Colonel's shop, challenged him for his base assertion, and called him '*farabutto*': though sounding such a deadly insult in Italian, it watered down in English to 'scoundrel'. This so incensed the explosive Sicilian blood of the Colonel that he rushed at Joseph with a 'scissors', causing the ignominiously small nick in his finger. Joseph, trembling with mortified, snipped pride, swore he was going back to break him in two. Since the merest puff of wind would have scattered the Colonel, like a pinch of dry pollen, back to his beloved Sicily; I did not think this was a wise course, and managed, with difficulty, to dissuade Joseph from it. By now the cold was unbearable, and though Joseph, warming up to the injustices of his part, was prepared to go on indefinitely, I had to bring the fascinating interview to an end. We had two quick, shivering glasses of wine, and set off down the path together. It was impossible to be angry with Joseph any longer, he was so deliciously serious about a thing of no importance; to salve my conscience, I explained that I forgave him, not because I believed him: I knew all about his '*onestissimi*' lies; but because I loved him. Having made this portentous confession for me, which slid off him, like sand off a fish's belly: he had no doubts about that in the first place; he answered, 'I love you,' to me, in exactly the same matter of fact way as 'Pass me the bread'; which was a great compliment, as he was inordinately devoted to bread.

As we neared the town he hung back, saying he dared not go in till it was darker, as the Colonel had threatened to put the police on him. He was in deadly earnest about it; only the joking suggestion that he was afraid: since he was afraid of nothing, except snakes, and would much rather face a lion; made him agree to accompany me, though he did not like the idea of me being his bodyguard either.

I always liked this kind of hour when the glaring part of the day was over, and I could pass almost unnoticed among the people: up the stone slabbed market street, where the long ghostly sheets dripped from the windows; past the close together, one after the other, nearly empty, rarely drinking, wine shops; the gargantuan hanging, shamelessly spread, animal corpses now decorously sombred down; and surrounded by a misty profusion of green stuff, glow-worm tangerines, pale bananas. The bright food shops, never still, and always packed with insistent, basketed, arguing for dear devil's life, black men and women. The now naked marble tables, still wet and stinking from the early morning sticky pinnacles of glistening, slithering, lively fish: sometimes one enormous one, covering the whole table, that the people gathered, in an excited knot, to watch being skinned; and the awful human baby face that was revealed. Last of all, and best of all, the pancake shop: in the warm half light, with the wonderful red blown coals, illuminating the big oven, where the pancakes were slid in and out, on a long handled slice; and shadowy figures stood around, mouths watering. And the verminous cats, and the scavenging dogs, crept close, anticipating the remains, ready to pounce, like starving wolves in the night.

Then, God help me, there was another dance at the end of the next week: by all the laws of what is done and what is not done, I had had my fling; I should have given it a miss, but there were two insuperable reasons that made it a point of duty for me to go. One was the visit of the velvet gloved, sister policeman, advising me, with the most touching concern for my welfare: whenever, like The Church, they had something thoroughly unpalatable to say to me, it was always solely for my sake; not to spend so much money on the wrong people;

to which I replied, Who, for instance, Joseph? Joseph, who was painfully punctilious, and, since he would accept nothing, not even a match from me, I smoked his few saved cigarettes out of spite.

At the mention of a name the policeman closed up with official embarrassment, and explained at gushing length, that he did not want me to go back to England with the wrong impression of the Italians: that they were all parasites, only interested in my money. I assured him that I was very fond of the Italians, though they seemed divided in their opinion about me; that they did not drink, so how could I spend my money on them; and furthermore, I had very little money, and that was not mine. In any case, I had spent it all on myself, and now it was nearly gone. He obviously attributed this mock modesty to the ravings of the mad English, but when I finished up with: And did you get all these instructions from The Church?—since he used the identical expressions; he put on a sudden show of deeply offended dignity; with a not terribly convincing: How could you suggest such a thing? But I pursued my advantage, hoping to turn the tables on him, called The Church and said to him: 'Is it not true you told him to give me this lecture in order to frighten me into doing what you want?' They made a prettily hedging pair of concerted denial, and both left very soon after that. I had not seen The Church, with a face of beatified grace, worshipping the buttons, arm in arm, up and down the street, for nothing.

So, if I did not go to the dance, it might appear that I was intimidated by the law and that would never do; and the other impelling reason was the mysterious tall stranger, who had danced with me so beautifully: I could not help being intrigued by such a paragon; had I imagined it, or was it true, that between us there was a surprising harmony. Would he be there? I was enough of a woman, in a very limited part of me, to have to find out; and had he felt anything special for me, or was I just another easy-going tourist to trundle around?

All the auspices were against it, and I was very sensitive to such phenomena: a thing that hardly ever happened to me, I thought I might be sick at any minute; and the tables, instead of being full and jabbering, were bleak and half empty; and the cold was awful in my bursting cotton dress. But he was there, and that was all that really mattered to me then. It's a funny thing but when the desire is on for one particular person, nobody else will do; and illogically that person may be of no importance ever again, except at that urgent moment. I was stupidly muttering, 'Please God let him be there, please God make him dance with me;' he was, and he did. He told me his name was Orlando, and I wondered how much more romantic he could get, with his half closed eyes, and low drawling voice saying: 'You are beautiful;' and me being wilfully fooled, and waiting, almost hoping for the flaw in this much too flawless for me, work of art. Then he told me he worked at Porto, which was the most wonderful place, I had discovered all by myself, and regarded as my very own, right at the end of the cliff, where the road stopped, and the daringest, last-of-all rocks jutted into the sea; and an eternal, heavenly land of almonds, heather beds, and, I had thought, salt-blown, unsullied by man, solitude, began. He asked me to meet him there the next morning, and so mesmerized was I by this scrap of unsolicited happiness, and because at night everything seems simple and possible, I said, 'Yes.'

But when the morning came, without any clear idea in my head, I automatically set off in the opposite direction to Porto, round the reverse side of the mountain, loaded with my usual basket, boots, sweaters against the cold;

185

and against the absurdity and incongruity of such a clandestine, and because prearranged, stilted meeting. And, though I owed Joseph no obligations, except that of secretly loving him too well: that piece of senseless weakness, I was trying to exorcize with all my strength, not with remarkable success; yet I could not bring myself to coldbloodedly deceive him. If only he would not look so heartbreakingly poignant, as he stood at seven o'clock on a drizzling morning, his face pinched white, and woebegone, under the peaked cap, his food packet clutched tightly under his arm; waiting for the Pullman to plunge him, and all the other jocular loud greeting men, into his drowning tunnel. And me pinned behind the slatted shutters not daring to show myself; only longing to take him in the warm dawn bed, hold him tight, and comfort him; while he imagined me enviously, wallowing in the lap of hotel luxury, without a care in the world. Lying in bed till all hours, with nothing to do all day but wander idly through the town and the countryside, mildly and pleasantly diverting myself!

How little he knew me, my character, or my fortune; or the ugly hole of my future that gaped at me with oafish vacancy, from the reaching nearer every day, annulling shores of England. Every now and then I thought, 'I have driven myself to the limit, I can't keep this up, I must pack it in.' But, having painstakingly cut all the cords, with the old Dylan-infested life, there was no alternative, nothing to go back to. Rio was the whole of my new life, and that was rapidly becoming out of hand, insupportable for me; or, to be more correct, I knew they would not support me much longer, and I should have to go, though I did not want to. Even my other children, who were perpetually gnawing into my conscience, and gave me a knife-turning pain to think about, were indissoluble from Dylan, and that other plague-shunned life, dripping with sodden associations and melting nostalgias. And, though Joseph, quite rightly for him, craved a modern, moving civilization, and was prepared to deny the red dust of the island for ever, I hated to think of his initiation into the so-called wider spheres.

And The Church; even more impossible to imagine him transplanted, his roots trailed, vine entwined, in the crusty earth, dragging him back. Sometimes, to amuse myself, I tried to envisage him in a London pub, a New York saloon; what would he do then with his bigoted code of dormitory deportment? And, above all, what would he do with himself? He would fit in nowhere: walking, lost, with a look of injured pride and com-miseration mingling in bafflement, on his great brute mug. With what love I would fall on him in those desolate wastes.

And I, reversely, wanted to sink myself in this so-old-that-it-stank civilization. I wanted, not just to walk on these age graven, gnarled, grooved mountains, but to be devoured by them; to faint in their hungry, pungent breath, to be mauled, and masticated in their sharp teeth of bushes, brambles, biting briars; to be swallowed, swooning, down the red cratered throat of their savage survival. As, indeed, that morning I nearly was, by going in the opposite direction to Orlando, finding a new, pristine, shapeless as pre-creation, land; losing the thread-of-pebbles path, falling into bottomless holes, landing in tangling undergrowth: clinging tenaciously to my skirt, stinging viciously my legs, my hands, my face; and, miraculously, finding the path again. After that it was as concisely laid out as a map, as long as I could read the indications. I arrived, at the end of the giant curve, at a transitory shelving place, where the water dribbled into pools, out of the rocks; and blue irises made it magical. A little further up, to my joy and amazement, I joined the top of the Calvary. I could not help reflecting that had I been accompanied, I would have noticed none of this; and though nobody, better than I, knew the pains and occasional lifts of solitude, I should have sacrificed all this hand-carved beauty, for one slap of humdrum affection.

It was in these 'Christ in the Wilderness' settings, where everything was there except the 'Christ'; as I sat on a flat stone, eating bare bread and drinking the mountain moss-sweet water, from cupped hands; that I felt less despoiled, but very rarely serene. I never sat back and tranquilly looked at things, I noticed very little, but they seemed to enter into me, in retrospect, just the same. I was over-obsessed by the monstrous image of myself, gnawing rodently behind the blinds of sight, that dragged daily its grotesque limbs laboriously, as far away as possible, out of sight: the sole purpose of its absconding was to be out of sight. I had a sad satisfaction in having had that amount of sense left, not to plunge into more trouble, and meet Orlando; it was not so much that I wanted him, but that I had still a terrible sense of sacred duty that I must try everything, with whatever disastrous results, if only for the education of finding out.

I knew I loved Joseph; he was much easier to love because he had a distorting need, an overpowering want distinguishing him from the apathetic normal: not for me as a woman; he was disappointingly undemanding at times; but for the world I represented to him. And so long as it was an impersonal game it was 'child's play'; but was it? Not for me; and to hurt him was like hurting a child, ripping my heart out. He had all the child's weapons of retaliation, with all the cruel time in the world, and callous, understanding nothing, conviction, to keep them up, and rub them in. I do not know what right he thought he had, to allow him so much temperamental liberty, but whatever it was, it was not for that I loved him. The things I loved him for were the things he hated in himself, and wished to forget quickest: his powerful, unavoidable, no praise to him, native Italian; some sweet spirit, which had all the charm of difference, and incalculable quality in it for me; his touching blend of wise melancholic maturity, with youth's unsuppressible bubbling up of fun, spontaneity, affection, appetites, which all his tunnelling serfdom could not keep down. His guitar, which he played with the selflessness and concentration of a dedicated saint, travelling in cloudy spheres beyond mortal comprehension; and producing an obscure, tuneless strumming sound. And his undeniable attachment to me; and who was I to question the contributing sources behind his attachment? It was enough that he thought I was worth his attaching himself to; and, gullible as always, though I had no confidence in my powers of being loved, I believed he was genuine.

With Orlando no such sensitive complications came into play: I saw him in the rival bar, as I was having a drink with Pietruchka, and at once I started to apologize, to make jumbled excuses for not being at Porto; but he was very sweet about it. He ordered some beer: it was the first time I had seen the extraordinary stuff in the island and, out of curiosity, I had some too. It was a rare treat, after the glut of wine I had poured regardless into myself; and brought back, with a gurgling rush, the turgid, thunderous, smothering years of Dylan beer drinking, which, try as I would, I could not smash.

Pietruchka disconcerted me by tapping his forehead, and pointing to Orlando, to show that he was simple. Now this could, or could not have been true, there was nothing to prove that he was or he was not; but it was certainly a very feasible explanation of my attraction for him; and once the suggestion had been made to me, I could see him in no other light. But I decided it was immaterial to me, so long as he danced the way he did, looked the way he did, and felt about me the way he said he did.

This was what they called the season of Carnival and Masks; hence the orgy, for Rio, of the dances; before Lent closed down on all unseemly revels, till Easter. In spite of their tepid version of the masking ritual, it still held the remnants of primitive fascination for me; but it was mostly only the children, and young boys, and an occasional adventurous girl who took part; scattering down the street in random groups. The most important thing was to be unrecognizable; so the richer ones bought conventional, cardboard, unimaginative masks; and the poorer ones just muffled, wrapped, tied themselves up in anything they could find; and made holes to see and breathe through, with much greater dramatic effect. They made a shabby crew of dubiously sexed, lunatic, magnified out of all proportion creatures: bosom and bottom ballooning boys, stuffed up with cushions and straw, wobbling and joggling from side to side on their top-heavy women's shoes; the shiny black petticoats rustling; the rosy lemon shawls fluttering, the frilly, flowery paper parasols twirling, or coyly dipped. The devil men, the black men, the saddest of all satin harlequins, with velvet buttons, proudly paraded by the moneyed mothers; and some strange grey hooded phantoms, who had simply covered themselves in a blanket, and fastened a cord round the middle, and who could pretend to be nothing at all.

I had an illicit longing to join the visibly invisible throng, without anybody knowing, and mystify them all with my dashing impersonation. One of my legion faults was that I was never able to grow out of the childish whims I should have grown out of a long time ago; and I still, in spite of the consistent punishment meted out to me, wanted to excel, to be the best.

I even went so far, in my yearning to dress up and be someone else, as to borrow an enormous baggy suit from the Englishman, and a desiccated panama hat, which I smuggled stealthily into the hotel in his black gladstone bag. I hoped, when the moment was ripe: the revels at their height, the masked rioteers in full swing, frightening the sleeping night into bad dream life: to join quietly in the crowd and nobody be any the wiser. Then have the gloating joy of revealing my identity later. But the moment never was ripe: the carnival just meandered on half-heartedly, in dribs and drabs, over what seemed weeks; and there was no peak to it: it fizzled out in a drizzle of wet coriandoli.

Because, of course, it always rained if there was any question of festivities, God saw to that. At the last dance, Orlando, more beautiful than ever, in tight black, from miles apart, head to foot: walked past me. A little later I saw him with a blonde, or was it two, clinging to his arm. If there is one thing I am very bad at taking, it is a slight: it takes me a very long time, in the first place, to understand that I have been slighted; and when there is no longer any shadow of a doubt about that, it is more than I can bearably endure not to know the reason why, and forthwith thrash it out on the bloody carpet. Was it the women who had driven me out? This was most probable; something he had heard about me from the cacklers, grossly exaggerated, and possibly connected with Joseph? I could not shake off my deeply injured pride, though I danced with extra abandon with the few down-and-outs still willing to dance with me, and I was grateful for his Lordship's grace in not leaving me partnerless.

I passed my Joseph, temporarily forgotten, sitting, a disconsolate clown with his mask slipped sideways . . . more lost than any of the rowdy children sliding between the dancers across the floor. Even Colm had come for this last occasion and was wilder than any of them. Joseph looked at me with a mixture of contempt and terror, and, did I mistake, a glint of envy? He rivalled The Church with his terrible looks, and could hold an offended dignity mood, impervious to prostrate persuasion, for days on end; and I noted, in a corner of my transitory sailing by, 'I shall pay for this tomorrow.'

Then I was conducted back, ceremoniously, by the full strength of the Beard family, and had got to the top of the flight of stone steps leading up into the hotel, when I suddenly got an overwhelming desire to go to the sea; and some unknown, unprepossessing, uncalled-for man, tried to stop me; up came the blind surge of rage, and I pushed him all the way down the stairs with me on top of him. It was a steep hard fall, and I was bruised and shocked, and hysteria started to rattle through me. The Church was there, and I held on to him, to, on thinking back on it, the horror of the family and neighbours. He carried me up the stairs, and I was put to bed; then I started to cry, in the good old gasping style, and I was right back where I had started, in the jelly pulp. A doctor came, and gave me an injection, and I got to sleep with a ring of nebulous, but darkly interested, and very voluble faces, staring at me.

And so for the shortest, delectablest spell, I lost touch with the outer world: time and reality were blissfully mingled; only too soon to come poking their sharp cold noses at me again. And those beastly ochre suns, behind their sprigs of mauve lilac, leered at me from their smeary clouds, off the walls; as though theirs was the last sky I should ever see.

XVI

MONEY was running out on me, and shortly afterwards,
ran out altogether. It is true I was going through it, as
though I could not breathe freely, till I had uncontaminated the air of its unsalutary presence; but I was
not worrying unduly, as I knew I had a fairly large
dollar cheque and a very small English one waiting to be
changed; and these would keep me going for as long as I
cared to look ahead. When the bank said they had no
authority to cash them, and I must wait, I was impatiently annoyed, but not seriously worried, till the
waiting lengthened into weeks and still nothing came.
And then, as my confidence waned, it seemed as though
all Rio was drawn together, in a tight knot of suspicion
against me; and I, who had given so liberally and
thoughtlessly before, went to the shops in trepidation,
and chalked up with false bravado in the café, with the
watched sense of the marked criminal.

I had depended on The Church as a certain source for
ready cash, but when I went to him it was not so easy: he
said, a shade shiftily, he was a little straitened himself,
and I knew his business was not as flourishing as he liked
to pretend; so he eked out the barest sustenance, totally
insufficient, for me. Then he refused to give me any at all,
and I was without a five-lire piece to rub against the
next; and anybody who has experienced this demoraliz-
ing situation knows the importance of the merrily
jingling coins in the pocket. Nobody more so than

LL—N

Dylan, whose whole horizon was lit up, or extinguished, by the presence or absence of the wanton, always insufficient, crinklers.

Plainly, without mincing matters, The Church was blackmailing me: either I did as he said, which primarily meant cutting out Joseph altogether, and got paid for it; or I persisted in my evil ways and got nothing. There was no doubt who was on top now: and being the Fascist bully that he was, he made the most of it. I played for time, I would not give in to his conditions yet, though my position was hopeless. I banished myself from mankind, trod the Calvary, and prayed hard for something good, out of nowhere, to happen to me; but my prayers were not answered, and my predicament grew worse. I even went to the Englishman, since I had no other friends I could ask for help, to borrow money; but I might have known that, being really a Scotsman, he also was living on a wangle and could do nothing; though I like to think he would have, if he'd had it. So I started to work up a proper panic at this too late stage, and for the first time thought seriously of getting out, getting back, and wrote a few desperate begging letters to my long neglected friends, whom it seemed I only turned to when in trouble.

I was impotently trapped, unable to go forwards or backwards; and, with the responsibility of Colm on my conscience too, I was persecuted with worries; especially at dawn, which is a well-known worrying time; and I did not know, with all my conjecturing, what I should do next.

Then, as though I had not enough mundane perturbations of the mind to contend with, the *padrona* of my house in the country: my only icy micey refuge; came back, clucking and cackling, and virtuously switching her tail feathers, to tell me that I must go, that she wanted the house back for her husband. He was such a useful man, that husband, if he ever existed; if he had any sense he would remain 'at sea', which I suspected him of doing. She used him as the instigator of all her bitchy remarks: as she alighted on the rotten gate, split in two by the wind, and scrabbled in the garden for the missing chain, which had been gently lifted by a strolling *vagabondo*, she prefaced all her remarks with: 'I would say nothing myself, but my husband, he is so fastidious.' And she industriously wrote down the item, and the price, in her reluctant account book. I let her have her head, knowing she had no hope of being paid, so she might as well have the satisfaction of rooking me on paper. She was evidently enjoying herself, as she swooped on the smashed window pane, missing cutlery, broken crockery, lost pots and pans, vanished glasses: mouse corpses in the ashpit. The mice had moved in overnight and taken possession with their machine-gunfire technique. I could pick nothing up and put nothing down, they had sprinkled their filthy droppings over everything, without exception, even the beds; and made of this squeamish indoors their pillaged province. I came out feeling untouchable myself, and, in an excess of exterminating disgust, bought a dozen traps which I set distastefully in their dirtiest revellings. Hence the dented corpses which, in my revengeful zeal, I had tipped, in vilely piled, visible proof, before the narrowed eyes of the Padrona.

She gave me one day to clean up and go, and since I could not face the job alone: I did not know where to start and it would have taken me a lifetime; I asked the Signora Beard who, because she laid herself down to be trampled on, it was very hard not to, to help me. She obligingly agreed, as I knew she would, and said she would come up in the afternoon. So I went up in the morning to clear a few preliminary dumps, and make ready for the onslaught of turning inside out, stirring up, and frenzied much better left alone polishing. I was sitting outside, at the table, in the precious bit of sun, enjoying for a moment that I thought was all mine, my litter of bread and wine and cheese and salad; when in walked the Padrona. And, as though that was not hellish enough, she was followed by a cortège of strange women: I counted them, there were a dozen or more, with several stray children thrown in. After saying: 'Buona Sera,' with that charming lilt, they all lined themselves up along the wall, watched me, and said no more. I tried very hard to go on eating and drinking unconcernedly: this was one of the occasions I was determined not to be outstared and cowed by them, and for once this blatant inspection did not affect me; whether because, for a miracle, my body was relaxed in this second of heat, instead of being as usual tensed against the cold; or whether because there is a limit to reacting to calculated torture, and mine had been spread on too thick lately, I could not say; but as long as the sun warmed me, I would not be disturbed. However, as time went on, and they remained as statuesquely un-melting as ever, offering no comment, the bread began to stick in my throat and I heard myself, to my extreme annoyance, making automatic polite remarks. I was by now fervently praying for the arrival of the Signora Beard, and at last one of the harpies spotted her, brave and small and absolutely reliable, coming along the sea road; I was never so thankful. She came among the villainous horde with that wonderful Italian insouciance that sees nothing, but is organically aware of all the parasites under the skin. I presented her to the Padrona, I am sure the wrong way round, as I never can learn who should be presented to whom; and my *dear* Padrona gave her the curtest of nods, as though she really was the charwoman; and as though, had she been, such rudeness was permissible.

Now my blood was up, which always solved my troubles one way or the other. The great thing is to know *what* to do, not whether it is right or wrong; just as the worst perplexity is *not* knowing what to do, which had been mine till now. Once anger had taken over I knew precisely what to do: I went straight up to the Padrona, and in my speciality soft manner, asked her to clear out, with all her ladies, or we should get no cleaning done. And, such is the power of believing in your own words, that very shortly they all trickled chirruping out. And then the Signora Beard, who had not missed one subversive intonation in the proceedings, set to, with a blind fury, assuring me she was only doing it for me, and not for that 'antipatica' Padrona; while I followed, like a useless idiot behind her, marvelling at the speed and assurance of her.

So one more prop was taken from me, and I was left to languish on credit in the palm of my grubby hand hotel bedroom, with hostility, and unpopularity, and suspicion, brushing, like a hard broom against me, as I passed in and out, from the family. It had come to the point where I was stuck for a means of filling Colm's school basket, and was forced to bring him back to the hotel to eat, much more expensively, on credit. I had run out of animal laxatives, essential cosmetics, cotton wool: the so-called small things which are, when one is deprived of them, very large things. I had never been so cold or dirty: not a single bath in six months, which was why I went into the sea, till I could stand it no longer: in my life before. Still I kept away from The Church and he kept away from me, and I said to myself: 'This can't go on, something must be done.' I had ceased to want the sun; I had become impregnated with the harshness of the island, inside and out; and I knew that if suddenly, as happened in these Latin, volatile climates, the country was transformed, with no transition, into a flowering, singing, appeasing spring, I should be undone, and never move again. But I was dead certain it was waiting for me to go before beginning to blaze, and blaze, and blaze, with no respite.

Then, in a deadlock of hoping, the American cheque did come through; do things ever come at the very moment we want them most? and as I doled it out, as fast as I could, it seemed to me the faces of the people round me changed too, and I was smoothly re-established. Although it was quite insufficient to cover all my debts, I felt I could survive now a few more weeks of comfort-less agonies: nothing really compares with the agony of having nothing, and by this time my 'money myth' was wearing a little thin. However, I had behaved, while it lasted, in a normal to me, but to them shockingly abnormal manner, which would never have been permitted without the myth. To the elect possessor all doors are opened, but don't they slam them quickly when he falls? It is as hard for a poor man to pass through the eye of a corrugated bodkin as to enter the house of a rich man.

I was all keyed up to go, while still not prepared to contemplate what fresh 'pools of despond' awaited me on that stagnant English side. The only objection to my going was Joseph, and he got closer, and harder to leave, every day; and made it all the more imperative for me to leave at once, before I became helplessly foolish about him. Then it was his birthday, and it was impossibly brought home to me again that he was no more than a farcical nineteen. It was out of the question, intolerable, but equally undeniable; love proverbially having no respect for age, rank, or nice decorum of any sort. And this rôle of the wiser, in theory, older woman initiating the innocent boy displeased me immensely. I wanted to be taught things myself, guided, for once forced into subservience; and he instinctively knew a lot more about this scratch and maul business than I. But I couldn't go down the stairs of years to meet him, and he could not come up to meet me; so there we were, me on the landing and him on the ground floor, and there was only one thing left for me to do: jump out of the window, quick.

I was reluctant to strip the cover off us on a cold and frosty morning. So I lingered on, did everything with him with a destined finality, as though for the ultimate, ultimate, never again, last time. But there were so many last times, and every time we got nearer to each other.

And so, when I should have been following my frozen resolutions: no more nonsensical dilly-dallying, vain transitory emotions; the hard, straight and narrow, disenchanting path; there I was distractedly packing up a picnic basket for us. We met guiltily at Gigi's: Joseph had shammed sick to get the day off, and he also was loaded with foodstuff, which when we put it together, a ton of bread for him, and a gallon of wine for me: I could not think how I should live in England again, where wine was served like a precious liqueur instead of being used to wash the glasses out, as here; it was heavy enough to break the back of a donkey, and poor Joseph had to carry it. We had decided, or rather I had decided: because Joseph could never think of anywhere new, and if left to himself would still be taking me to the giant girdered pier, sticking out breathtakingly high above the horribly far-down sea; and consider that the uppermost platform of this wobbling creaking structure, on the bare boards among the clanging rafters, was a perfectly adequate and suitable bed for us; and all my country places I had found alone, and had to show to him; like the rest of the people living in the town, he was content with the conventional beat up and down the street and never dreamed, unless it was suggested to him, of penetrating into the jungles surrounding it; to go to the castle at the very top of a neighbouring mountain.

So we set off, with a guide to show us the way through the preliminary mined, excavated, gutted mountainside; and in spite of myself and against my will, I was becoming fascinated by the powerful drag of this monumentally ravaged, turned-inside-out intestined, rocky-bodied mountain mortuary; and it was like nothing so much, I swear, as an unfolded human body, with blood's own lurid colours. And again I could only think in paint: it was not there waiting fruitlessly to be painted, it was a live, co-ordinated composition, needing only an enormous sheet of tracing paper; how I wished that I could do it; for to be honest, I paint no worse than I write, but the materials are so much more cumbersome. Those pinks, and browns, and blues, with a flush of yellow and green, as subtly, and simultaneously as clearly, interwoven as a bird's egg, were as tempting as a box of American candy.

So much of the mountain's stony, clotted, red ironed bloodstream was being consistently drained away, in relays of heavy laden lorries, winding steeply to the widely mothering, from high up here miniature, cargo boat below, that I could not conceive how this undermined hulk of mountain did not cave in on us. And with all the chugging and trundling, and explosions in the heart of it, making a background thudding as buried as a heart beat, there was, as we passed the abandoned quarries, a stilled cathedral quiet. I felt uneasily estranged from my romantic country on the other side, lying there so peacefully unaware of this digging industriously working world. I was won over, bewitched by the strength and elemental beauty of it, that tamed my green groves into aunty's tea gardens. And I should have enjoyed nothing more than to be one flesh with these slaving, sweltering, supermen, and to work anonymously alongside them. But being wrongly sexed, wrongly coloured, and wrongly designed by nature in every possible respect; I was unfairly debarred from the things that gave me the greatest satisfaction.

Then we got a lift in a lorry driven by handsome Mario: long, black, side-whiskered, head tied artistically in a purple scarf: but there were so many like him, or even better, and they always gave the impression of indolently amusing themselves; to the inner side, away from the sea, and looking toward the layers of pastoral somnolence. I noticed, for the first time, that the vines were more like trees turned upside down in the ground, with only their roots protruding, than anything else; and that the broad beans, which, I seem to remember, are only planted at this time of year in England, were sprouting in rich profusion beside them, as though compensating, with their freshness, for the hibernating dryness of the vines. How was it possible to believe that those old tree roots would, in their own appointed time, produce welling, paradise filled grapes, from that stony unyielding earth; though, it is true, there had been enough rain lately to swell a paradise of fruit.

The constraint between Joseph and me had almost gone, as long as we were out of vigilant eyesight; though this was not strictly true either, since my constraint was walled in for as long as I can remember, and it would take an eternity of patient loving to break it down. But by Joseph being so much himself, so natural, and so undoubting: and this is not to say that he was not complex; he instilled into me some of his confident spirit, and I found myself, to my surprise and gratitude, unconsciously responding to it. We even had silly jokes together, and I laughed a gurgling-up laugh, which only just avoided being a giggle, an indication of our besotted state. And the very absurdity of it, knowing it had got to end so soon, made it that much more attractive: this giggling adolescent, deadly serious drama, with the unforgettable arch of Dylan dwarfing us, and creating worms out of our seriousness.

After some time, as we went on walking and got no nearer to our castle receding mountain, I saw, far away in the distance, a very small, ancient church, shrouded in mist, which Joseph told me was Santa Caterina. So, of course, I could not resist going to see my posthumous church. The day after Easter, he told me, from all parts of the island, the people came to celebrate her, in a continuous merrymaking cavalcade, and stayed all day round the outskirts picnicking, making music, making love. But these descriptions of Joseph's of spring and summer merry-makings to come: the inrush of chattering flashy plumaged tourists, without a care in the world, letting themselves go; the brightly striped umbrellas, the family parties, the punctiliously modest undressing, the coy, calculated to ensnare, disportations on the beaches; the lights, and the boats, and the serenatas into the night; gave me a nasty twist in the stomach. I could not bear to think of him enjoying it all, thoughtlessly, without me, and still less could I have borne to witness his faithless boy's enjoyment. Though it had very near slain me, I had done right to come in the winter: happy crowds of laughing people, invading my private sanctuaries, would have been harder to endure than all the island blizzards put together. Holiday romps were not for me any more, if they ever were; I had gone too far backwards, into the ratty runnels of my beginning. I knew I must go, but shut my eyes to the impending separation, the animosity rounding up on me, and the damp disillusion in the stagnant trough of England.

At Santa Caterina we sat among the stones, toying with tantalizing fairy-tale ideas about Joseph coming to England, and working there, then going to America. It became more and more impossible, but impossible to leave him too, after him saying to me: 'You are my only hopeless;' being smartingly nearer than he suspected to the truth.

It was not only the declarations he made so captivatingly, because he had not yet learned to barb his feelings, but also, and perhaps more so, his 'innate' capacity to hurt, and I, who had thought myself beyond hurt, was hurt by him: I could feel the hurt passing recognizably, and pleasurably: because to feel something nameable is better than the nameless nothing; through my body; and his fierce, jealous pride filled me with admiring wonder, and wonder of wonders that I could inspire it in him.

The evening before this particular Sunday, The Church had threatened to throw me in the street if I ever spoke to Joseph again. And it was the night before that I had come in late for supper, and he had turned on me rudely and said he would not serve me at that hour, and I had walked out saying I would not eat then, and went to the bedroom to reflect what to do. But with a child, as mothers to their sorrow know, these acts of vainglory are not so easy, so in five minutes I was back again asking, with biting politeness, for one spaghetti and one orangeade. He brought two large dishes of minestrone, the orangeade, and my wine, and it was with the utmost self control that I resisted touching either of mine, but drank a glass of water, the first over here, watching Colm. My refusal of food in Italy made a deep impression, and later in the night when I was in bed, he crept into the room, threw a meat sandwich at me and slipped my wine on to the dressing table; for which act I felt I could forgive him all his manhandling of me, and never truly stop loving him. On the Sunday after all these accumulated upheavals, Joseph had made a very special plan for us.

He had gone to the touching trouble to find a house way beyond, and even deeper in the country than Santa Caterina, belonging to a very old uncle; and he had bribed him to clean it up, and build up ready a stack of wood to make an enormous fire in the vast grate, as I was always moaning about dying with the cold, and no fires. There he proposed we should go early in the morning, and spend the entire day till nightfall; cooking our food in a flat pan he would bring along, drinking, resting replenished on the sofa by the fire, making lessons. He said nothing about love. This idea both attracted and frightened me, as I have a superstitious terror of planned enjoyment, especially when the unpredictable element of love comes into it, with the no-getting-out-of nausea of a honeymoon. I foresaw pitfalls of personal embarrassment, and a failure on my part to react, to do the right things at the right times; to give the light, easy, warm, casual intimacy, that such a rustic escapade required. But on the other hand, I was burning with curiosity to see it, and it has never yet occurred to me to deny myself a temptation because it might do me harm: that stipulation is, if anything, an irresistible challenge, an added incentive. My only real concern was Colm, who would spoil all our delightful make-believe if he came with us, and it was too far for him to walk; but I could not think of anybody I could leave him happily with, that long: they all wanted their pint of grown-up blood, would have done it willingly knowing me to be on the verge of dissolution, but at the scent of immoral enjoyment, and most certainly guessing Joseph to be in it, they clamped tight to their house rocks, like insulted limpets.

Babbo Beard was ill in bed looking long since dead, as though the removal men had simply forgotten to take him away. But he was still eating with the hunger of the nearly dead, and giving martial instructions to the family between coughing fits: I wondered which of us would go first, to our drab, dismal, overcast homes. In the end we decided to take Colm and Chico together with us, so that they could play outside, while we got on with the work inside. And it all seemed perfectly feasible in the simplifications of the night.

We walked for a long way along the clean sea road, as opposed to the iron contaminated mining side, without saying anything; or me venturing a fatuous remark about the lovely day. The dreaded transformation had taken place, and all nature expanded like a lazily awakening beast; I chided him gently about not appreciating the beauty beguiling him in vain, of wasting the precious gift of sudden generous sun; to all of which he answered not at all. I could feel him physically tautened against me, till his sustained silence steadily dragged me out of the sun, into his dark, wrathful captivity. Then, with a rush, he burst into a flood of Italian abuse; just as I had to resort to English when I was in a terrible temper, and bound to swear; about his marathon injuries on my account. His early rising on his only day of rest, his noble lonely, long trek, his reorganizing, and putting to rights of the house, his exhausted run back, panting, because he thought he was late to meet me, obediently waiting on the dot of eleven. I began to say how sorry I was, that I did not realize, I had no idea ... but to all my hopeless protestations he kept repeating: 'False liar,' till I felt, impossibly, that I was going to cry. He made me so miserable, and I wanted him so much, that I asked him please to go if he was going to go on being so horrible, and refused to be nice. But he was not content with leaving me in peace: he had not yet had his full mortification out of me, to assuage the imagined affront done to him; so he hung on, for the sole purpose of making me suffer, as much as he had.

We came to a cactus bed, not the prickly kind, the squelchy kind, and I lay down, shut my eyes to the encompassing sea, and tried to forget him; he planted himself silently about two yards away, and did not move. Not able to sustain the oppressive enmity of his personality, boring remorselessly into my consciousness, ruining the wonderful impersonal day, I stretched out my hand to him, hoping, by the physical contact, to overcome the snakes of suspicion and mistrust devouring him. But he was as repelling as the brick wall which had reared itself unbreakably between us; he shoved my hand rudely away, and said he did not want me. I gathered up my things and said I was going, but he did not want that either, and would not let me pass. We stood locked together in exasperated, speechless combat, then we fell down on top of each other, and he blessedly began to laugh: as though brick after brick of the wall was crumbling between us. But it was only a half love he gave me, with the bitterness still riling him; and when he got to his feet again, shook back his wild lank hair from his distraught, greenly glinting eyes, and buttoned himself firmly into his tight jacket again, he was already reassuring himself with his cruel wrongs.

XVII

I HAD got another house by this time from Anna Maria,
the breasting daughter of the café below, on the mining
side of the town. She spoke of it as though it was in the
deepest country, but actually it was only up the opposite
eternal steps, a short way along the top of the cut-all-
shapes-and-colours cliff; with the lorries perpetually
pounding past the door, to unload their heavy cargoes
into the trundling jaws of the machines, that conveyed
it ceaselessly along the pier, and into the hold of the
great patient barge, which, it seemed, would never be
filled, and must surely sink to the bottom. Till the
puffing steamers came to drag it to mythical places,
across the water, far away. Although Anna Maria's family
must have been sodden with money, and they owned a
lot of the property round-about, yet so strong was their
training for making more, and the tradition of continual
work, more especially for the women, that they never
stopped slaving in their café, and complained of never
getting a day off, or seeing the country. Only Francesco,
the father, who had the biggest belly in Rio; also, I
discovered to my surprise, possessed a soul. On my distant
wanderings I would come upon him, standing stiller than
a scarecrow, in the midst of his sheep, contentedly
pondering: not, I trust, on his digestive organs; and
when I passed again, a long time later, he was still standing, in the same position; and said, in explanation, he
liked it better there.

The house I had taken was a deserted ramshackle vault, with none of the intimate charm of the other one, though Anna Maria was unreasonably proud of it; and I was made to admire the big, high-ceilinged, gloomy rooms, with only a stripped iron bedstead, or monumentally polished wardrobe, in them, and boarded-up windows. The kitchen, for some obscure reason best known to itself, was perched on the very top of the roof, like a dove-cot, and always kept locked: I imagined a ghostly cook scattering her garnished dishes out of the broken window, like pigeons. There was about the whole place, with its large straggling garden, and glut of exotic scented, mating flowers: —Anna Maria said the lighter and the darker purples exchanged pollen to make the screaming magenta between them; and cosy pink geraniums, a—melancholy, reminiscent air. I was told later by Mister, who never knew when to keep his mouth shut, that it was the house where we all went that last time, with Dylan and the family; and I began to remember, reluctantly, where we sat, under the usual vine climbing trellis, how hot it was: and we were drinking wine of course, and Dylan was talking. Was he ever not talking? though in what language I cannot imagine, because we were certainly among Italians. Even The Church was there, but he was not The Church then, he was beautiful Giovanni; and just as he wished I had not come back to ruin his beautiful memory of me, so I could not help being struck by the solidifying, and not glorifying, difference in him.

Whenever an outside voice spoke of Dylan, as opposed to the constant inner natterings, and in Rio it was a safe rarity, then my fragile edifices of self, of important functions, of love: above all of love; came toppling, with the insubstantiality of card houses, on top of me. When Joseph told me that I was vain, boastful that I was the most intelligent person here: and that would not be so difficult; I was complacently flattered that at least I had successfully achieved that contradictory deception. As for love, I could only think of it not in connection with Dylan: if I thought of him, if I dared to look at one word he had written, and worst of all to me: there was one letter which, whenever I went to get out some impossible official document from my wallet, stuck itself out and cried to me: 'I am profoundly in love with you, the only profundity I know. I love you Cait, only you, now and forever, I love you with all my life. Oh, I love you so much, Cait, think of me as I think of you, with all my body and heart, your Dylan for ever'—my subsequent loves shrivelled up like Valentino's kiss with the match-sticks, and wilted away in black cinders. I was not even sure that I ever had loved Dylan, but I was beginning to suspect that *that* is what it was; and if it was not love, it was something overpoweringly stronger that killed outright any other experiment with love. All this emphasis on love from me, who had never bothered about love before, was because an invaluable love had been taken from me, and I was at my wit's end to know how to replace it.

I spent three of the bitterest March whistling days in that heatless, heartless, haunted vault; being relentlessly whipped back, from my shivering table outside, into the cold unwelcoming rooms. And at last, as the rain slashed viciously inside, I had to close the outside door; and there I sat, in the afternoon twilight of my meeting weathers, thunder and lightning booming and flashing round me; and I concluded that when adversity is piled on thick enough there comes a moment of exaltation, of rising above circumstances, of not caring what happens next.

When I met Joseph again that evening, by the disused

prison: our new meeting place on the mound, now packed with families jabbering under the high windows; he was more serene, but the black blood still throbbed spasmodically in him. But it was its very blackness that, unknown to him, attracted me. He still insisted that I was false, had played him up, made a fool of him: the universally biggest fear; my only fear was that he would sense the forbidden extent of my love for him. He obstinately went on saying he did not believe me any more, that I was a perfidious woman, and when he had made me thoroughly cast down: 'Did I love him?' I went on just as obstinately repeating dully, 'Yes.' Then suddenly he smiled unashamedly, gave my cheek an affectionate Italian twist, and a sharp smack; and said he was only testing me out, and was now happily convinced I was telling the truth after all. It was my turn now for a little blood to start boiling.

By nightfall our ranklings of near hate had simmered down: we met for the usual coffee after supper, and strolled idyllically up the still, stony road. He was talking impetuous Italian, which it always seemed to me he talked better than anybody else, and, though I understood little it was a pleasure to listen to him. He had the gift of being completely absorbed in whatever he was doing at the moment, to the exclusion of everything else: he ate, talked, made lessons, or love, with his whole heart, body, and soul exclusively. As we neared the hotel, as innocent as two pontifical doves, The Church barred the doorway with his massive, malignant bulk; I said to Joseph: 'I know he is going to do something awful now to me,' but Joseph answered airily: 'Don't you be afraid of him, he is only straw fire,' and he walked casually on, leaving me to face him. I went up to him, said: 'Excuse me, can I pass?' and, before I could get any further, received a stinging blow in the face, and was slung off my feet inside the door. My first reaction was incredulity that he dared make such an exhibition of himself in front of the gaping public; accompanied by snarling vilification of me. I hesitated to fight back, for once not in the fighting mood, and more concerned than he at the disturbance, not for me, but for his impeccable name. I tried to reason but it was no good against his flood of invective, so, at an unfair disadvantage, I stumbled up the stairs.

To be met at the top by his wife, who had been standing there all the time, quietly observing us. I muttered some protest about his extraordinary behaviour, but she merely shrugged condescendingly and said: '*Troppo confidenza*,' too much confidence between us. . . . I made for the bedroom and locked the door.

He had ordered me to have all my bags ready packed by twelve in the morning. There were no limits now to the unreasonable excess of his avenging vanity. He had never been seriously, or consistently, crossed before, least of all by a woman; and the experience was contrary to the most solemn laws of his Church. But, in seeking to humiliate me, he was dealing with a substance that he did not understand: impossible for him, and a Fascist, to understand the absence of fear: the metal that they hammer into their own image. He could inconvenience, upset, make living in the island 'impossible' for me, distress me; but not, no never, frighten me.

He incanted mournfully his old history of my wrongs: I paused to consider how much truth was in it, because there must be some truth in every swollen tale. Was it perhaps true that I, whose mind grated rustily against the enveloping tissue, was the monster I was made out to be? What was I guilty of, what crime had I committed?

I was guilty of loving a young boy, but that was hurting nobody as much as myself. More obviously, I had neglected Colm, half because I could not help it: my predominant mother's instincts had died along with Dylan; half deliberately, because neglected children are unfairly always so much better. I do not mean I starved him; I saw that he was fed, clothed, washed; the bare minimum essentials, but I gave him none of my concentrated personal attention, so important to a child, so they say, but they don't know me. I left him playing recklessly in the streets, with the wild street gangs, while I went off to the country on my own, putting my faith in feckless chance that no fatal bodily harm would befall him. If the harm was no more serious than learning the bad language, and dirty words, which shocked the good people to the roots of their shuddering beings; he reeled them off at the most inopportune moments, while I sat by blandly unmoved, understanding nothing; I was not as worried as I ought to have been.

Though I was taking a big risk with him, I could say that he was not unhappy; not that a child is ever consciously happy or unhappy. But the bottling up, hermetically sealed suffocation, the lonely imprisonment, the airless isolation, in a house with two old ladies and himself, imposed by the Englishman on his son; with enough pampering and cosseting and fussing to nurture a whine of hypochondriacs; and terror of this and terror of that, and don't, and keep aways, and come backs, and wrap-ups, and go to beds, and take the temperature: that household Totem pole that makes an awesome tabulation out of a common or garden flush or high colour; was, to my way of thinking, a far greater crime against the human spirit. And as like as not, so capricious are the machinations of fate, he would be the first to fall down a pot hole, so unaccustomed would he be to dodging them.

But this is irrelevant to the final orders I was curtly given by The Church, sticking his judicial head into my room at dawn, before I was arraigned for battle: to have my bags ready packed by twelve o'clock, when he would return to remove them. He sounded as though he really meant it more than ever this time. I said nothing, with great difficulty, as there were so many things I could have said; and, it seemed to me, the only thing to do was to proceed as always, and get away as far as possible, if not even further. When at the end of school I returned to the Albergo, with involuntary misgivings, I saw that at least the streets were clear of my disreputable trappings; but in my room the cases had been thrown pointedly on to the bed, as a heavy hint to start packing. I threw them as pointedly back on to the top of the wardrobe. We repeated this manœuvre several times, without once saying anything about it, till in the end The Church gave up, and I heard him holding forth about the hard heads of the English.

XVIII

In the middle of these skirmishes, the telegram came, summoning me to England, and settling up, with not very good grace, the essentials. I did not know what my reaction would be: I knew I had to go, and I thought I wanted to. So many things in England pulled and repulsed me at the same time, but the repulsion was stronger; though my children tugged at the dangling cord, and there was no saying no, there was no choice. So I surprised myself when I took the envelope, fingered like a dead mouse, along the mineral shores, and opened it tentatively on a rock, with a gulp of panic and tears.

When I next saw Joseph again and told him my bomb-shell news, he was outwardly singularly unperturbed: impossible to conjecture what went on inwardly, that was the fascinating part about him; simply said we must spend as much time together as possible, make some beautiful outings, in the last few days; and he asked for four free days off from work. Since they were only allowed twelve days off, with pay, in the year, and he had already taken six of his: they mostly saved them up for the intolerably inviting summer; it was no mean sacrifice, but I was not satisfied. I wanted to hear him say again, when I talked of going: 'It is impossible,' with his halting ambitious accent on the wrong syllable, making it indeed impossible for me.

We had two days of near harmony, with the accompanying diminuendo of stimulation. Then we went, at last, by a blend of cunning and subterfuge, to Joseph's uncle's immoral house in the hazy mountains. It was one of those days when, by some extraordinary oversight, all the wrong things: blowing raw noses, blistering cheeks, hands cramped dead in the gloves, toppling shoes, straining, clinging, indiarubber skirts, billowing, bulging, wind-pranking coats, and the total atrophy of all the finer senses—did not happen. God was slipping, and the weather was milder. Although it could not be contended that we were completely at ease: the inevitability of our actions was weighing too heavily upon us. We went on: and on: and on eternally: I began to think Joseph had made up the house, into this strange, vaporous, immobile countryside from the long past; and came to the house in a valley, under the road. It was a typical primitive stone hut, with a giant black key to open the creaking wooden door. Inside was dimmed by the tiny sealed-up windows, but I could see indications of vigorous brushing on the flags, neat stacking of rusty utensils, and a big pile of firewood by the elevated grate: Joseph's brave efforts in the very early morning. We were nervous and trying not to be, and not sure what to do next, keeping an exaggerated distance apart. I suggested making the fire, and in no time Joseph lit a crackling blaze with the dry wood, and we were enveloped in great gusts of sooty smoke, which steadily grew thicker. But it served to alleviate the tension, as we blundered and stumbled about with smarting eyes; and I unpacked the basket, and sat in a smoky corner, and started to drink the wine. Then we found an old pan, poured about three inches of olive oil in the bottom, and a lot of salt, then chucked in six eggs, and pushed it into the smouldering embers. I was ashamed to show Joseph how little I knew about cooking, with his high standards at home, but he was very good-natured about it, and not much wiser than I. When we pulled the pan out again, having temporarily forgotten it, there was a solid yellow lump floating in the oil, which, when I spread it dripping between the long loaves, was the best thing we had ever tasted, we both agreed; and it really was delicious.

And now with the filling and warming of our stomachs, the burned patches from the guttering fire, and Joseph's birthday sweet: a rich concoction of creamy cherries and sticky pastry which we mixed with wine to make more interesting; we began to feel better, to laugh, permitted ourselves a brushing 'mother's' kiss; and went to lie on the torn, tattered, holey, damp sofa against the wall. As I held Joseph sleeping later, restless, tormented, groaning to himself, pushing against me, and his imprisoned oppressions, I felt nearer to him than I had ever been, with a love that was, at that held and passing duration, purely detached: as unrelated to my cringing needs as Colm's golden, football-faced sleep, which asked for nothing, except my whole, undivided, immortal life. So I thought, with three young lives already clinging fast to my lopsided, wavering, wave-agitated raft; because there was no other perishing raft to cling to; and when there was, I should be scuttled fast enough; I must help this boy.

And so I bluffed and romanticized my rôle; and how had I saved this boy except by adding to his discontent? But I could not, would not, believe it would end there; there had to be a continuation to this serial, it was too fictitiously engrossing to drop.

So I rose, padding barefoot, looking for my boots and bits, in the smoky wicked, incriminatingly sun-pierced room; while Joseph went on sleeping, as though he would never wake. The day after, as we wandered, listless and chastened, up the half-made new road, he spoke with a fatalism as sunken as that same somnolence, which baffled me and went against my whole nature; untrained to accept, like him, the inexplicable calamities and griefs that fell out of the sky, with no apparent discrimination. I fought hopelessly against them, and still would not, could not, never would accept my unacceptable grief.

And likewise I hated Joseph's acceptance of unhappiness, his resignation: I wanted to shake a protest out of him, when he calmly said: 'I shall never see you again, I shall go on rotting in my tunnel for the next forty years, till I am finished and ready to die'; I wanted to kill him for it. Then he would visit all the places we had been together in, lose himself in our languorous ghosts, and be content in only remembering, wishing for no more. This was useless talk to me, I wished for no more than his live body against me every night; and the memories, the nostalgias, the yearnings: I already had a bellyful of them, there was room for no more. For once all his defences were down; with my inescapable and plodding nearer departure, our actions were paralysed at the dying root. The time was passed for playing up, testing, tormenting, the jealous garlic of love. Joseph laid it on rich and dripping, he was charming, disarming, too much wonderful, as he once said about me, to my consternation; I could not help feeling that his Italian eloquence, which flowed so liberally, so poetically, and somehow so meaninglessly, was carrying him away from me. I stood rigid, powerless to stop the wash of soft soap lathering us apart. I wanted to cry out, to stick a knife-edge into his impersonal rhapsodies which, it seemed to me, had nothing to do with us, could have been said to anybody. Make him cross, make him flip me, if necessary, just pleasantly hard on the cheek, as he sometimes did, in offended indignation. Anything but this sincerity of

217

undiluted sweetness, which left me cast away alone on my Caitlin cranky, cantankerous, coruscated, cruelly corroded rock.

That evening, like rooks and crows cawing their disasters in their yelling heights, there was another funeral. Lately there had been a daily succession of funerals: the old people, of which there were an inordinate number in Rio, were dying off in a rush before the summer, as though the winter relics were being recklessly discarded. I was constantly running to the window at the sound of the blaring brass band, expecting some new celebration; only to see the familiar procession of swaying pale madonna; clucking hen priest with his clutch of solemnized boys; same old tatty, tinny, red-ribboned, laurel-leafed wreaths, held toppling aloft; the casual stragglers varying the afternoon monotony, tucking away their butt ends, baring their heads. And somewhere, always somewhere, hidden or seen, the little economical box. Death was determined to push its trumped-up smallness under my nose, as though its pervasive stench was not already rotting my nostrils.

Pursuing the beetle burrowing trail I went with Rita one day to the Catholic cemetery. She was the middle daughter of the Beards, one year older than my daughter, but, though outwardly a similar compact, well-planted type, there was a race of difference between them. Rita, a woman from the day she was born, never a child, with a professional sense of responsibility, shaped purposefully in the sole expectation of her unique function: to serve a man and his family. She strode undaunted, body-welcoming, into her secondary, static rôle. I recalled how she had sat all day at my bedside when I was ill, scarcely moving, and thought nothing of it. While Aeron, my girl, spoiled, wilful, immensely self-centred, lived in a child's exploring world, fabulously magnified, with no confines, and the oppressive shadow of womanhood but a far distant threat.

We walked round the high slab-walled enclosure, going back and back, reading the names, and looking at the photographs stuck on the outside, of the permanently retired inhabitants. So many Giuseppes and Giovannis, uncles and aunts, nephews and nieces, and cousins of The Church and Joseph, telling me I did not belong, and never would belong. Some were gruesomely cemented into the wall: the stone was removed, I can't think how, the bones of the previous inmate, if over ten years old, were thrown into a large communal coffin above: which also presumably got emptied after a certain period, though I don't know where this dusty blend of powdery personalities was sprinkled. The new, shiny, fresh-from-the-world coffin was slipped into the narrow cavity, and the stone put back with a different name and photograph. Rita and I agreed we would rather rest in the central plot of friendly earth, with the trees and the flowers round us; but even this nearer the light alleviation did not seem to me as delightful as Rita made it sound, as she went into ecstasies over her fairy tale underground. I thought, thwarted, again: 'These Italians, I shall never get near them.' I wanted my bones to fly from the mountain tops, in all windy directions.

As we came back towards the entrance a heavy smell of heady half-spent blooms, waxy candles, and something else, came to meet us. By the side of the door was a glowing chamber reserved for the most recent arrivals, and there was an air almost of a recent party inside; recent emotions stirred and throbbed, charged with prayers, fear, and the mass excitement of the slaughter-house, that had so overwhelmed me in Chicago. This was the ante-room of death where the last classifications were made, even in death the classes must not be con-

219

fused. The rich to their family, cold-storage vaults, white marble statues, and embossed plaques; the poor to their wooden crosses, their crowded plot, crammed together like they were used to living, with the jampots of withered flowers. The artificial pasty concoctions under glass, the Catholic stage properties.

Then we wandered off, silent with our separate fears, through the bamboos, and the soapy streamlets, and the solo man always working in the groomed fields, with the women bringing him food; to the tiny church of San Giuseppe, Joseph's church. We ate sour oranges, picked daisies, and cracked the hard almonds with stones, coming back to the watching town filled with our joined truancy.

Then, on the nineteenth of April, it was San Giuseppe's day, a holiday, and above all a day for Joseph, so we naturally wanted to do something together. We missed the twelve o'clock bus because of the usual prevarications and palavering with The Church; so when I met Joseph in Gigi's later he was cross from waiting about all morning for us, and would not speak to me either. By trying to please too many people and acting inconsistently, I managed to offend them all. We walked off, bristling with unsaid injuries, towards the mining beaches: I tried joking with him, he was icily not amused, there was not a glimmering of a smile; I tried to distract his attention with lengthy discussions on English pronunciation, spelling, usually a sure subject of absorbed interest; there was no response, only a stony silence; I gave up, we walked on stiffly, saying no more. We serpented down the craggy cliff, our feet sliding from under us; we sat on the iron stained, rubbly stones, with a foot of arctic snows between us; I kissed him clumsily, because I minded too much, he was apathetic, not protesting, but as hard as frozen mutton; then suddenly

220

he leaped up saying I could do as I pleased. I stayed where I was, not moving, watching him flouncing off so convinced of his own rightness, and concluded how much better off I was alone. But after lunch, dreading the prospect of a windy resortish town on my own, with no idea how to get back, I went down with Colm to the café to wait for the two o'clock bus. There was Joseph smiling, affable, just as though no wrinkle of dissension had ever furrowed our sunny relationship; we followed him obediently up the road to anticipate the bus.

Once inside, speeding away from the critical eyes and nagging voices of Rio, with the squeeze boxes playing with holiday jauntiness at the back, I felt a sudden lift of spirits, a blessed sense of not caring about past or future that comes so rarely, at such unforeseen moments. I made that prodigious leap, over that library of time, to my early days in Ireland, before descending into the oyster light of marriage. When I did things, not because I had to, because there was no alternative but to do them; but because I was under the quaint misapprehension that I was unique, especially chosen to fulfil a great, if somewhat ambiguous mission. So I brought to my every ardent activity a dedicated intensity: how was I to know I was dedicated to child-bearing? The buzz of the Irish concertinas and harmonicas and flutes and fiddles came back to me, out of the back of that Italian, tame imitation bus; and the muted surge and delirium of the blood trickled through the locks of the years, and tickled my spine. And just as I only grasped afterwards the happiness in that misty distant, innocent, humming with summer and bells, and the Falls Ennistymon, first chapter; so now my happiness in this Italian bus was gone before I could reach out, to grab at it. Before I knew where I was, I was on the street, creeping away with Colm to the windy out-of-season beaches, while Joseph went to look for his friends, the old men players, to create '*divertimento*'. He had arranged for them to meet us in the morning, and now we were two hours late.

We lay for what seemed a very long time with the white-sugary, tourist sand blowing into our eyes, and the willowy apologies of trees sheltering us; till Colm spotted Joseph with a tiny, teetering figure, tottering under a top-heavy load. They came slowly nearer; I could see Joseph was worried by his friend's unsteady condition, which in England would have caused a kindly smile, but in Italy caused a shocked gasp, as though the poor man was lost beyond redemption.

We moved on to a small more sheltered bay, after sending Joseph back for a *fiasco* of wine: he never could understand the necessity for wine at all hours of the day; and the old man, who had mislaid his senior partner in the long winey wait since morning, sat down on a rock and, with meticulous care, unwrapped his older-than-himself concertina from its tattered cotton rag, and started to play, terribly fast, a wild jigging tune. I was so starved of music, much more essential than reading to me: a food as essential as bread and wine; that I was intoxicated, hypnotized, prepared to sit happily listening to his dug-out-of-his-youth melodies for ever. Then Joseph came back with the wine, we drank, and he settled himself, as complicated a process as posing for his portrait, with a borrowed, decrepit guitar, and began tinkering and tuning with absorbed intensity. It was one of his beautiful days, and I gazed at him, knowing he was impervious to me then, trying to retain intact the sad passing vision of him. But his taut playing would not combine with the old man's feverish fingering and squeezing, and a set disdainful look of annoyance settled on his face.

Colm too was getting bored by this time, and throwing

himself off rocks into the water to draw attention to himself; and the old man kept dozing off and nodding over his concertina; so we broke it up, and wandered roundabout back to the town, leaving him in his musical sleep.

The small enchantment vanished as soon as we got among the holiday noisy knots of conjecturing people, and the worldly self-consciousness of identity and suitability returned. We went into a café, sat disconsolately drinking tea and coffee, mine automatically laced with cognac, robbed of speech, though we had been gabbling quite happily before. Then it occurred to me to ask when was the next bus, and I learned, to my dismay, we had just missed one and there would not be another till ten o'clock. All my motherly fury rose up in defence of Colm, who was dropping on his feet, and had got to the unendurable whining, petulantly, twangily, nasally wheedling stage, beyond bribery or corruption; or even Joseph's patient charm; with a fixed obsession that demanded the bus, and the bus only would do. So, in despair, I turned on Joseph, and remonstrated indignantly with him for not telling me about the cursed bus times. I could see a look of terror come into his eyes, common to every man, in my acquaintance, when he thinks his woman is going to make a scene or a show of herself. But in spite of seeing clearly that I was doing irreparable harm to my romantic status, I could not stop, and for that very reason piled it on even more; and proved once again that the rampaging mother beast, in a crisis, is unsquashably uppermost.

After walking abortively up and down a few times, as though in a secret conspiracy, we came, quite by chance, on Rosso: big property man and driver from Rio, who agreed to ditch his job for half an hour, to take us home, for the sake of that shining bait, a wee bit of extra cash. Notwithstanding that he was one of the richest men in

Rio, with a posh luxury villa on the uncontaminated side, and owned a fleet of lorries. But so much second nature had the sacred habit of money-making become with him, that the fruits of it were secondary; he could not spare the time to enjoy it, the fascination was in the money-to-money begetting. So we arrived late, and dazed, and carried Colm up the street like a sack of passed out, snoring potatoes.

As we stood quietly and tiredly chatting at the foot of the Albergo steps, deciding where to meet tomorrow; The Church darted out of the café next door, ordered me curtly up the stairs, and told Joseph rudely to go. Joseph advanced on him aggressively, answering back and gesticulating. Nothing went more against my nature than to walk out on an argument, or a brewing-up fight; but with phenomenal strength of character I dragged myself on, up the stairs, for I was sure in this case my presence would do more harm than good.

I had scarcely got to the top when I heard a shattering crash, and a splintering of glass; and, a few moments later, The Church opened the door a crack and whispered with fugitive urgency: 'I threw a bottle at that *cretino*; but he escaped; it will teach him a lesson, I will tell you more in the morning.' And he was abruptly gone.

XIX

Now there was less than a week to go; then only three days; and still I had not the courage to clear my dumps of clothing in various stages of dirt; bundles of letters, papers, miscellaneous refuse collected through the anonymous hotel months. What to keep, and what to throw away; ending in an excess of disgust, with throwing the lot out. I had in equal proportions a horror of possessions and a greed to acquire more; to start my packing, and rip the wound of my going. And, as though to gloat over my going, in the little ever-diminishing time left, the sun shone with a permanent smug grin as much as to say: 'I am here for keeps, I am not for you, and get out!'

And in case God should seem to be slacking, at His ever-vigilant tasks, and giving me too much respite, He turned Colm red and blew him up like a mottled blotchy pumpkin. So, instead of being able to hurry him off to school in the morning, to have a last few precious hours in the flaunting countryside, I had no alternative but to keep him in bed. I was torn with compassion for him, ludicrously unrecognizable, though quite cheerful, and I wailed inwardly, knowing the insuperable difficulties of keeping a child in bed who is not positively dying: how were we going to weather the bedridden stretches of day, to kill the demon time?

The evening before, I, not to mention Colm, had gone through a gruelling experience with his tooth. We had

LL—P

both been putting off the fearful deed for as long as possible; but it worried him badly at night, and we could not leave it any longer, and I was afraid it might get worse on the journey. So when the short, round, jolly doctor was up in Babbo Beard's house giving him his habitual injections: injections were prescribed regardlessly for any old complaint, they were all the rage, and served to polish off the patients as efficaciously as most remedies, and a prick faster than nature. I asked him, not too confidently, would he do Colm next, take out his rotten tooth? He agreed, but said we must hurry as his dinner was waiting. So we all, including The Church, who had come to do the accounts with me, as a plausible and constant excuse, and which oddly never got done; trooped down the steps after the bustling doctor to his surgery.

As we got near to the door Colm hung back instinctively, like cattle smelling blood outside a slaughter yard; the supporting children vanished, and I was left alone with The Church, for whose rallying presence I was very grateful then: tugging, pulling, cajoling him, while the doctor went ahead to prepare his incisive instruments. Seeing my trembling nerves (I was afraid I might be stupid enough to faint), The Church offered to take Colm in on his own, but he wanted me: mothers must not be allowed to escape any of their children's sufferings. I knew only too well it was one of the ordeals that had to be done personally, though this was one of the true occasions when I would have infinitely preferred it to be happening to me, and not to him. We went into the naked, greenish lighted room, sat him on a stool at the foot of the surgical bed, and held him tight between us. The doctor tripped over, tapped his teeth shrewdly, exclaimed: 'Ah, yes, this is the one;' and, only just in time, I pointed out; and insisted, that the bad one was at the bottom, not at the top. Quite undeterred he responded: 'There must be two then, we will take them both out,' and again I had to insist: 'Just the bottom one for today, please.'

So he approached with the tweezers hidden in his hand, and Colm panicked and struggled, but he swore there was nothing in his hand, and he was only looking. At last Colm opened his mouth doubtfully. Thereupon the doctor jabbed his hand in, clutched at the tooth with the tweezers and pulled with all his might. Needless to say, the tooth did not come away with the ease of a pea from a pod, as they always like to pretend; but resisted, and crackled, and spurted blood. Colm screamed as piercingly as a stuck pig, as we held him down; and the doctor pulled him up; and we seemed to be pulling him apart between us. When it did come out in the end, and he was choking with blood, sick, terror and pain, we discovered there was not a drop of water in the surgery to wash his mouth out; and he was too far gone to let the doctor disinfect the cavity; so I had to carry him back to the Albergo in the deplorable state he was in.

It was no wonder therefore, when I saw the metamorphosis of him in the morning, that I thought feverishly of blood poisoning. The Signora Beard insisted it was mumps, which were prevalent in the town, and it certainly looked, with his monstrously swollen, scarlet face and neck, suspiciously like it, and I almost believed her. It would mean, she said, at least eight days in bed, and I groaned 'God Almighty', while a tiny, disgusting voice exulted: 'You won't be able to go now.' But the doctor denied it, said it was nothing, only a minor indisposition, and prescribed a pile of expensive and useless pills: with no method on earth of getting them into the child, as usual. Pastes and purges; the latter were the most effective; adding airily, as though it was the easiest thing in the world: 'Just keep him in bed for a few days.' I got very cross, and asked him if it was nothing, why did Colm look like he did?

But after two or three days of bedroom squalid farce, with the bed awash with:

> Aranciata,
> Tea,
> Broken biscuits,
> Crumbs,
> Stuck-on sweets,
> Distended or balled chewing gum,
> Squelched pools of sucked fruit,
> Bricks,
> Comics,
> Mechanical toys,
> Boats, and
> Beard children,

Colm gradually deflated and paled down to his normal colour; it was too late to bother to send him to school again: there was a bare week-end to go, and we were to leave at dawn on Monday

XX

THAT last Saturday, I was neither in Italy nor in England, I stood still and stubborn between the two unrealities saying: 'No, no, no, I hate, I hate, I hate, and I won't, I won't, I won't.'

But I could delay the start of my conclusive packing no longer. I sent Colm tottering, still palely mottled, into the too bright day, and, among the ash and Aleatico, the cinders of my already receding visit, I began, with the utmost distaste, pulling out drawers, throwing armfuls of unnecessary clothing out, attempting all thumbs to fold them, pressing them furiously down in the trunk that there was no hope of shutting. Every now and then going to the window to stare down into the street: there was the oaf boy, whom I had reported to the police, calmly plastering the house opposite. Further down the street, longer, more beautiful, distinguished and distant than ever, in the special Rio soft working boots, with hat pulled down over his eyes, Orlando. Samo, The Church's soppy son who disliked me, or, I preferred to think, disapproved of me: disapproval being a bit more flattering and a little less incomprehensible than plain dislike. Eolo, who used to be the friendly illiterate waiter in the Albergo before he broke his arm crashing on his Vespa, now growing fat on contented idleness, coming out of his bakehouse all flushed and floury, like a baby out of a hot bath. Nacco, who was surely the oldest man there; not counting Babbo who was, strictly speaking, not in this world at all, simply paying a last-minute call; bent double under a gigantic sack; he was probably the strongest too, and one of the poorest; his contemporaries sat all day, in all weathers, on a bench in the square, gazing and waiting for the earth to open and swallow them up; he was always begging for five liras, which he spent on wine, getting chucked out of the cafés, being knocked about, having his hair, which grew like a fresh mown upright grey, hard lawn on his head, brushed the wrong way, cigarettes stuck in his ears, his nose tweaked; and he made a fantastic old-man-shaking act with his scabrous hands, especially when asking for money, but never spilled a drop of his drink. One day of raging blizzard, I asked him to carry a sack of small coal for me over to my house, and he plodded doggedly, unmolested by the tempest, a measured distance behind me; when we had climbed through the driving rain, sidestepped the whipping wind round the house, and he had dumped his load in the mouseridden kitchen, he turned on me with a leer of unbelievable and unbelieving craftiness, and asked me, with an amateur threat, for a thousand lire. For a joke, and because God overdoing it again put me in a foolish mood, I gave it to him with no argument; he nearly dropped dead with shock; and a genuine expression of panic, at his hamming succeeding for the first time, came over his face, and he darted for the door before the spell broke, and I snatched it back. For a long time after that he avoided my company, and slunk away guiltily whenever he saw me; he also did less work, and drank more wine.

There were the conducted farewells to be done, and Joseph was rightly nervous that I would drink too much, over-reach myself, go too far: put him to shame, in short, never mind about my welfare; but, he could not have been sweeter, he warned me to go easy, to go slow.

But there is that about well-intentioned advice that has the opposite effect of the one intended, and causes a Spanish fly of perversity to enter into the hitherto passive soul. Thinking myself in complete accord with his sagacious sentiments, I went with him to the 'Merry Widow' first. She was in the same abandoned ship as me, only she carried black-as-pitch sails all the way up from her feet to her chin, whereas mine were multi-coloured. There I made bright talk, and told gilded lies about buying houses, bringing the rest of the family across, and setting up a posh establishment for us all in the summer. By playing up to the myth of my easy circumstances I had come almost to believe in it; and these wishful fantasies of mine, I convinced myself, were actually in the realm of possibility. But if ever I had the courage to look homewards, and saw, through the blinds of my unwillingness to go there, the heaven-rent, wrecked, wracked shack, adrift with water, and manned by rats; sunk in the leaking navel of Wales, that once was my home when Dylan in those far-off, still near days, slept there; and now was less comfortable than a crucifixion: then I knew it was no good pretending any more. I did the big gesture, bought wine all round and paid for the double popularity of spending money, and going away: an infallible combination. I took down addresses of people I should never write to, made lavish promises I should never keep, expanded graciously in my queenly affluence; when, truthfully, all I was doing underneath was clinging to, fighting for, but losing, my disappearing straw of resurrection.

And so, nonsense on nonsense, to Gigi's, where we repeated the same procedure, perhaps a little more fulsomely; and Joseph was beginning to look a little worried and unhappy, perhaps the way I liked him best, and I was beginning not to care. A group of my table neighbours at the Albergo: the higher up executive workers in the imperative mining business; tonight, which was a Sunday, day of feasting, were all jollity, smiles, and lascivious glances. I sat down and joined them, which was perhaps another not very wise thing to do; and Joseph looked still more unhappy.

Then Mister jittered in, as neurotic as a poet in his dark glasses with gabbling speech: he irritated Joseph so much that he practised his assiduously learnt, but only half-assimilated, 'standing phrases' on him, and said confidently to him in English: 'You are a pain in my neck, go and toss yourself off,' to which Mister replied, with his smattering of Americano: 'O.K., Jackass,' as amiably as ever. And I was the only one understanding who was a little discomfited.

The nobs were waiting uptown, and at last I detached myself: it was both laughable and deeply touching to me that I, who had played the reformer for all those years with Dylan, telling him what to do, and what not to do, trying to temper his indulgences; should now have a boy who could almost be my son, following me about, trying to keep me in order. To add to the absurdity of the situation, there was The Church, if I strayed from the respectable rendezvous, sending out search parties to rescue me from the down-town vice rings. Once before, when we went to look for a different café solely for the purpose of playing music; and installed ourselves; Joseph, me, Mister and Ernesto; in the dismallest cavern, as empty and encouraging as an out-of-order public lavatory; on the unfashionable side of town; and Joseph was grimly strumming, and Ernesto murmuring his fervours, while Mister and I sipped acrimoniously the vinegar white wine; the proprietor came up and whispered in my ear, then led me mysteriously to the kitchen, where I was at once set upon by frantic Beards sinister with forebodings of my dark fate. They had already scoured half the cafés in Rio under Dictator instructions from The Church, and they led me back to civilization, an unresisting prisoner between them.

We arrived in the select quarters, among the step-up society of the Colonello, the Englishman, the Doctor, and Church and his beloved buttons, the Maresciallo; Joseph slipped away, since they made it so obvious that his company was not desirable, and they could not tolerate him at their table. The class differentiation was subtly obscure since Pietruchka was tacitly accepted, though he worked in a tunnel like Joseph and came from the same kind of family; however, he was an adept at assiduously laying on the charm in profitable directions, whereas Joseph had rebelled since the day he was born, and was not at all popular with the high-ups.

By now we had got on to the old Spumante and a flushed sunset glow stole over the ensuing proceedings. The Englishman offered to come with me on the boat in the morning; we asked The Church to join us, but he was too afraid of his wife; and all the time I thought miserably: 'If only I could take Joseph with me.' But whatever the emotional pitch and conflict, the eating had to go on; and we dispersed one by one, as usual leaving the Englishman and me, the lonely Nordic survivors on a desert island. As, the souls of sense and moderation, the benign Italians politely left us.

When it was all over, and Colm was in bed, surrounded by an eruption of overflowing cases; and I was not feeling so good, and it was getting dangerously late, I made a wild dash to get out. The Church on the stairs held my wrists in a madman's grip, and forbade me menacingly to go. But I was as mad as he, and we stood locked together like fools; until his indominantly bovine wife, for whom quietly I had a great attachment and admiration, intervened, telling him to leave me alone, and what was it to do with him anyhow.

When I got into the nearly deserted street, the cafés were just closing, and Massimo was spreading sawdust on the floor, to brush out afterwards; I ordered a coffee and saw nobody, only Mister weaved and nattered round me, as persistent as a mosquito, repeating maddeningly: 'But where is Joseph?' as though *I* didn't want to know. As though our love had rolled itself up into a tight ball of mortification and longing that pushed us apart, and neither of us could circumvent it; and, outrageously, I had to simulate unconcern, to shrug and say: '*Non so*,' as though it was a matter of negligible interest to me.

We wandered off, round the going-to-bed town, pretending not to look for him, having last glasses of wine, being flippant, frivolous, falsely gay. But he was nowhere to be found, and a sickly lump of sorrow mounted in me, and lodged incontrovertibly in the middle of what I imagined was my heart. And I carried this bastard load with me back to the hotel, for inspection later, aware only that it hurt.

It was his wretched precious pride again: 'but there was no time for that now,' I pleaded into cloth-eared vacancy, and bit into the log of wood pillow. 'I will explain it all in the morning,' I thought, to comfort myself, quite forgetting I had told him not to come.

For to meet Joseph had become more pain than pleasure: we were so conscious of its finality that we could not enjoy it, and, like people on platforms praying for the train to leave to cut short their overloaded futilities, so we appeared impatient to get the worst over, and be left in peace to begin our serious long-term suffering. I had asked him would he please *not* see me off: thinking of that early hour harassed by bags, tickets,

234

money, all the inevitable embarrassments of bungling departure; and most likely a stunning hang-over on top of it. Striving, through this fog of petty details, to keep the purity of my love for Joseph untainted by them, flying bravely above them; to find the right words, make the only restrained gestures. I would doubtless fling my arms round him, never let him go, and ruin his name for life; and it was he, after all, who had to live there, not me, as he once told me. No, it was a too monstrous scene to create: it must be ruthlessly cut out. But now I had forgotten entirely the request I made of him, and I searched despairingly, with my eyes, among the people all like sudden strangers, not daring to make it too evident, for a sight of him. In the morning I could not believe he would not come, and the hardest thing was to drag myself to the end of that pier that struck horror into me; and not bolt back, storm his house, and throw myself into his sleepy bed.

Why did everything always happen at the wrong time, with the wrong person? And I cursed myself for always killing the climax: skirting round it, afraid of the peak moment, going to cowardly labours, destructive excesses, to avoid the final commitment, the pinning down, the binding declaration of faith. The permanence that smacked of death.

And why were the simple things made so difficult for me; why did I learn so slowly and laboriously, and painfully, the things that Dylan had in him already, without learning at all. The way he described a thing he had never seen, as though it had been with him all the time and there was no need for him to see it. I had the unenviable sensation that he had anticipated all this, and was lying down looking at me drowsily, with pitying love, and saying patronizingly: 'So this is what you wanted'; for nobody could be crueller than he when *he*

235

wanted, though few people suspected it; and I felt lower and wormier than the worms in his poems.

But it was no good thinking about Dylan: there would be his hands again, limp and folded, innocent sleeping: like a bloody baby; and that would start a longing on another scale. Not like the longing for Joseph, which was immediate and keen, with the hope of *some* satisfaction some time; though that too would be taken from me soon. But a longing which was bitter and baffled, but not beginning to be tamed, even in a year's pelting of stones on my head; and which had no hope ever: ever: ever; of seeing him again; except that I should always see him and re-create him through me. But there is no great satisfaction in that, it is no good saying that, not when you want the hot mortal body against you. And a wave of rage and revulsion swept over me for the insignificance of that death in November that caused so much damage and carnage: that I was not allowed to be present at, because I was in that place with the bars and the netting, camouflaged a tasteful grey. When they came shiftily to tell me: it was the flattest news I had ever heard. And cumulatively a revulsion against myself, for what I was, had been, and was going to be; the stale repetition of the last act. However much I turned, and twisted, and struggled, I could not avoid the tedious, but unavoidable process of deterioration, nor the bed of crawling vermin.

So to that crawling night, which was faster than sleep, and over before it had droppingly begun; which was broken into by the cruel Church, the importunate daylight, and the indecent hour of six o'clock in the morning. A monumental rock, the biggest of the lot, lay across my breast; as the nightmares behind and in store for me hurtled pitilessly through my brain. It was almost as impossible to move as that time in New York, when I

236

had to get up to accompany Dylan back, in his box, on the boat. As I lay in a trance of paralysis the room was filled with Beards, flustering, and fussing, and fuming to hurry: that I only had half an hour to do everything, and nothing was done. I got creakingly out of the bed, and began doing meaningless jobs: it was a pure act of mind over the protesting matter, which was clenched in a fist of negation.

Somebody pushed Colm into his clothes, I pushed myself clumsily and stickily into mine, and, as I cleared the decks of last minute trashery, the Signora Beard pounced on oddments, discarded too cumbersome garments, and stuffed them in a long capacious bag brought especially for that purpose. A quick gulped cup of boiling coffee, and we had *got* to go. The Church, who had quietly observed all these circular manœuvres, stood at the door waiting; I thought: 'It can't be really over yet, I can't leave him like this,' and I held him tight for a moment, wishing never to let him go, or to let myself go, imploring him silently. But as soon as I got into the street, with my cavalcade trailing after me, I could think only of Joseph, and where was he?

I had never, obviously, been up at this hour before, and had no idea there would be all this crowding and activity going on. We got all tangled up with the men going to work, and the buses coming to fetch them; and the café was flourishing and busier than in the nights. But in all these work-sculptured faces and work-beautified costumes, I could not spot Joseph in his poacher's outfit, with his basket under his arm, and his tragic-orphaned face, under his peaked cap. They dragged me relentlessly on; I bought tickets for the steamer; automatically, against my will, we went on to the pier. The row boats were taking over the first load of passengers; hope died in me, and I could not speak.

As they were loading up the second boat with my mountain of cases, the Englishman came strolling along in his Burberry and fisherman's hat, carrying a folder of Scotch schemes; as cool and detached as the perfect casual Englishman: and, as he stepped firmly into the boat, he said offhandedly: 'Bit of a near shave, that.'

I squeezed all the Beards, shook Mister's hand politely as though I had never seen him before, tipped boys distractedly, held on to Titi's sharp shoulder-blades till the last: he was the raggedest down and out, and his bottom literally was out of his pants, in Colm's gang; called: 'Arrivederci, Titi,' as though he was my only son, and my heart was breaking, which it was. The boat was rowed away from the pier: that pier that contained so many reaching out desires of mine, that lullabied of escape beyond the beyond; beyond the little horizon of my too in-turning world. I clung to it now, to every slippery flagstone that I could not get a grip on; and I felt, as we heaved up and down in the small shaky boat, that my body was being scientifically torn apart.

A single infinitesimal grace was afforded me: a faint drizzle, instead of a crowing sun; and it was too early, or they had overslept, for those nostalgically crowing cocks, that crowed up my youth; or else we were too far away already to hear them: there was too much sea between us. I stood on the bare deck looking through the mistiness, praying a useless prayer: 'Let me see him once.' Had he been there it was not conceivably possible that I could have seen him; but I went on saying it just the same. And when the sea became too wide between us I made myself say: 'I shall never see him again.' Now the drowning began in earnest: the waters broke over me, drenching me, as I still stood dripping and blinded, waiting for the next wave to knock me over. I saw Colm all blue, without a coat, his hair still undone; and, in my

238

bedraggled rat-tailed grief, I still knew it was a miracle that I had managed to save him: the living testimony, with so much of each, of Dylan and me; from the island where I had made my first steps in a new, dark world: that he was my scourge and my miracle.

The Englishman was being as good as gold, and doing all the right things. He answered all Colm's millions of questions, that I never knew the answers of, with punctilious exactitude; only remarking to me: 'You seem a little absent, my dear, you have not been listening to a word I have been saying: you had better forget about that fellow . . . he is only an Itie you know, and you are nearly old enough to be his mother.'

We landed on the mainland; and that longest of all mornings in the wronging world dragged on. We sat and drank bitter Campari which merely accentuated my deep depression; and Colm begged ceaselessly for money. It was the only thing, I regretfully concluded, that he was seriously interested in; his passion for it was shaming, and he was permanently jingling coins, which he extracted tyrannically as the price of peace, from everybody without exception. It was not the sticky messes that he smeared all over himself, the table, the chairs, streaking the immaculate plate glass window with his tell-tale signatures, that he cared about; it was the money for its own sake. I don't know from which hoarding Welsh uncle he got this acquisitive streak; because Dylan and I, though fond of the stuff for what it provided, were neither of us gifted in acquiring, or with the mean genius of keeping it.

At last over lunch he fell asleep in my arms; a grubby bundle of potentialities valiantly fighting against the dying of the light: my miracle. Gradually the afternoon wore shabbily on, through Mandarini punches: a new discovery of the Englishman's, adding heat to our emotions, and red-hot coals to the oppression of going. Then, with no fanfare, it was four o'clock, and time to go for our train. Controlling a lost impulse to break away, to do some violence, I embraced the Englishman, who backed away with a look of startled alarm; and we were handed up into the high-stepped Express, with the long-suffering bicycle following behind.

This is it, this is the finish, a beaten voice said inside me; and the train started to trundle, and chug, and drone:

Going home, going home, going home;
no home to go to, no home to go to, no home to
go to;
going home to no home, going home to no home,
going home to no home;
no home no Dylan, no Dylan no home, no
Dylan. . . .

And all the mountains I had ever climbed came tumbling down, and crumbled at my feet.

And all the king's horses, and all the king's men, couldn't put Caitlin Thomas together again.

FINITO